SECOND GENERATION

SECOND

HUNGARIAN
~ and ~
JEWISH
CLASSICS
REIMAGINED
~ for the ~
MODERN
TABLE

GENERATION

JEREMY SALAMON

with CASEY ELSASS

HARVEST
An Imprint of WILLIAM MORROW

HarperCollins books may be purchased for educational, business, or sales promotional use. For information, please email the Special Markets Department at SPsales@harpercollins.com.

FIRST EDITION

Designed by Tai Blanche
Photography by Ed Anderson
Food Styling by Spencer Richards
Prop Styling by Maeve Sheridan
Chapter opener star pattern © Tanya/stock.adobe.com
Stars, moons, and other doodles © Polina Tomtosova/
stock.adobe.com
Picture frames © Tartila/stock.adobe.com
Cream paper © Svetlanais/stock.adobe.com

Library of Congress Cataloging-in-Publication Data
has been applied for.

ISBN 978-0-06-331723-9

24 25 26 27 28 IMG 10 9 8 7 6 5 4 3 2 1

For my mother, Robin,
Nana Arlene,
and Grandma Agi.

Thank you for
setting the table.

Contents

Introduction

 **Csillag**

One of my earliest memories is of my little legs running up a four-story walk-up in Boca Raton, where Grandma Agi was waiting at her front door, calling out "Csillag!" She wore big fashionable glasses, a leopard-print housecoat, and fuzzy slippers. The apartment had a thick smell of frying pork cutlets, her rántott hús. She'd hand me a chocolate egg cream, usher me and my older brother, Jordan, into the kitchen, and feed us until we were plump. Dessert was almost always palacsinta spongy egg crepes that looked like yellow moons with brown craters spattered about. She let us stuff them with nuts, cheese, jam, sugar, and syrup. The evenings ended in the den where we would all watch *Wheel of Fortune* with Papa Steve while Agi would draw me pictures of fairy-tale characters wearing the most elaborate gowns and costumes.

Grandma Agi, my paternal grandmother, grew up in Budapest, Hungary, at the worst possible time, to put it lightly. She survived life in the Jewish ghetto during World War II, the Stalinist regime after the war, and the Hungarian Uprising in 1956, a failed attempt to overthrow the oppressive communists. After decades of hardship, Agi finally decided it was time to flee. On the night she left Budapest, she stopped by her sister's house to say goodbye. Her sister covered her in a big fur coat, and Agi slipped off into the night, headed for the safety of Austria and eventually New York City.

My paternal grandfather, Papa Steve, also improbably survived a war-torn Europe in the former Czechoslovakia. Nazis stormed his house and Steve was sent to a traveling camp, where one of the Nazi captains took a liking to him. The captain tipped off Steve one day, sharing that he was going to lightly staff the patrol that night. Steve knocked out a guard, took his gun and uniform, and strolled right out the front gate. He ran back to his village in the mountains and a couple hid him in their barn until the war was over.

In a happier time and a happier place, Grandma Agi and Papa Steve met at a dance hall in New York and settled in Queens, running a successful dry cleaning business together. (Grandma Agi kept that fur coat intact well into my childhood, so she obviously had a natural talent for garment care.) They raised a family and, like all good Jewish Americans, eventually relocated themselves (and their dry cleaner) to Florida. That's where I enter the picture.

Csillag is the Hungarian word for star. When Agi would call me csillag, it made me feel like my world was magical and full of wonder. As I got older, that sense of wonder started to fade. I was exploring my independence from my family and making my own path in the world. I found my way to New York and landed in some of the toughest restaurant kitchens in the city. If anything is going to knock the magic out of your life, it's working as a line cook.

It wasn't until I happened to find the last tattered copy of *The Cuisine of Hungary* by George Lang sitting atop the sale pile in a Manhattan bookstore that the wonder came rushing back. I had never seen a cookbook on Hungarian food, and I pored over its extensive history of Hungarian cuisine and culture; it was both new and familiar. There were illustrations of kings and queens in extravagant costumes stuffing their faces with palacsinta but also dishes I never knew existed! Chilled berry soups, hearty braises with ripe stone fruits, and layered cakes as tall as a person. All I had known of Hungarian food was fried meat and heavy sauces. I immediately purchased the book.

That day kicked off a decade of my own discovery of what it means to be Hungarian American. Being second generation often means a weak connection to the language, customs, and rituals that make you special and unique. I traveled to Hungary, living there and eating my way through my heritage. I convinced Grandma Agi to give me her recipes (although it took some cognac to coax them out). I layered my cheffy instincts over centuries of tradition. I found my own internal csillag, a guiding star passed through my family and into my own sense of self.

To the Moon

Nana Arlene, my maternal grandmother, was born and raised in the Bronx by Sephardic Jewish parents. She met her husband, my Papa Howie, in Rockland County, New York, where they ran a very successful pharmacy. When my mom was a teenager, they moved to Florida and reopened their pharmacy in a strip mall. Their next-door neighbor in the mall was a dry cleaner run by . . . Agi and Steve. Nana Arlene and Grandma Agi became chummy, and like good Jewish women, the yenta instinct kicked in, the photos came out, and my mom and dad were matched up by my grandmothers.

My childhood was A Tale of Two Grandmas. Both of my grandmothers are ladies who lunch, ladies who entertain, and ladies who fill up a freezer, ready to feed anyone who walks through the door. Wherever I went, I never lacked a good meal made by loving hands. In the summers, I would bounce between the comfort of Grandma Agi's apartment and the cool of Nana Arlene's country club. For a kid, it was the best of times and it was the best of times.

As I got older, Grandma Agi would shoo me out of the kitchen, even as I became more interested in cooking. She didn't understand a man wanting to cook; a man should be cooked for. Instead, it was Nana Arlene who began cooking with me—trussing chickens, baking chocolate cakes, and making peppery vinaigrettes for Roquefort salads. She is an exacting master technician in the kitchen. She saw that cooking was an inescapable part of me and was happy to be my first, and best, teacher.

My entire life Nana Arlene has said "to the moon," her shorthand for "I love you to the moon and back." I think of Nana Arlene as my moon and Grandma Agi as my star, the guiding forces in my life. It was ultimately those driving forces that led to me opening my own restaurant in November 2021. I wanted not only to make a mark in the city that had been a safe harbor for Agi and Steve running toward a new life but also to represent the cultures that they were forced to leave behind yet couldn't help bringing with them. Agi's Counter, tucked in the Crown Heights neighborhood of Brooklyn, is my homage to everything I grew up loving: Hungarian home cooking, Jewish deli counters, Arlene, and Agi.

Second Generation is not my grandmothers' cookbook, but it is my way of sharing a bit of their magic with you. Hungarian food is extraordinary, unique, and full of old wisdom. I'm reimagining those traditions with an eye toward seasonality, market-driven ingredients, and a touch of millennial flair—mixed in with some classics from the restaurant alongside a few Hungarian-inspired dishes of my own invention—because I want to help bring Hungarian cooking out of the shadows and into the twenty-first century. And all the parts of this book that lean distinctly Jewish are gifts from Nana Arlene. This book wouldn't exist without the two matriarchs of my family, my moon and star, who taught me that food and love are just synonyms for each other.

The classics are here, like Rántott Hús (page 89), Palacsinta (page 177), Meggyleves (page 61), and Chicken Paprikash (page 82), with small updates for contemporary kitchens, techniques, and tastes. The greatest hits from the Agi's Counter menu, like Deviled Eggs (page 14), Chicken Liver Mousse (page 17), Tuna Melt (page 50), Caraway Caesar Salad (page 104), and Chilled Buttermilk Borscht (page 58) bring a little taste of the counter into your own home. And my own reinventions, like Turnip Schnitzel (page 79), Smoked Trout Butter (page 19), Heartbroken Beets (page 120), Madártej (page 172), and Körözött (page 20), a Hungarian take on pimento cheese, are here to take a forward view of what Hungarian cooking can mean.

This book will guide you through noshing (the official fourth meal of the Jewish diet), breads, soups, mains, and sides. Because sweets are such a huge part of Hungarian culture, I have two separate chapters: one for cakes and tortes and one for desserts (there is a difference!). The drinks chapter takes familiar flavors in new directions, and the pantry chapter will help you stock up on staples that feel time-tested but still brand new. Finally, the remedies chapter is full of the things the matriarchs of my family made to comfort me in good times and bad. Throughout the book, I'll interject to offer helpful tips and advice, clarify ingredients, or offer alternatives. Just think of me as your own grandma in the kitchen with you.

George Lang opens *The Cuisine of Hungary* by saying, "Of the many reasons for this book, perhaps the most important one is to show to the rest of the world that this stepchild of history has an extraordinary and unique cuisine." That has always been my goal at Agi's Counter, and I'm proud to bring the same ethos to *Second Generation*. I hope these recipes will comfort, excite, and nourish you. I hope you'll cook them, share them, and adapt them. I hope they join the weekly rotation or provide the perfect finale to a special day. I hope they become part of the fabric of your culinary language. I hope you find the magic and wonder. And I hope one day these recipes turn into their own second generation and feel like something that's all your own. I believe traditions are meant to be shared, and I'm proud to share mine with you.

Egészségedre!

Notes on Sourcing Ingredients

Most of the ingredients in this book should be familiar to anyone who cooks regularly. And luckily for all of us, options for vinegars, oils, produce, and spices have become robust in most every grocery store if you need a restock. For the few things that jump out as unfamiliar, there are several options:

- Research your area for any Hungarian, Jewish, or eastern European markets. There are so many shared ingredients in the countries across the region, so it's a great place to start, especially for anything fresh.

- Farmers' markets are always the best resource for seasonal produce. Talk to your suppliers and see what crops are coming up. I love walking the stalls for fresh radishes, greens, peppers, tomatoes, herbs, and beets. The markets often have meat and dairy, and egg suppliers too, so might as well get it all done in one stop!

- For spices and pantry staples, shopping online is often the easiest answer. My trusted resource for everything you could ever want is Kalustyan's, a Manhattan landmark that also offers national shipping (foodsofnations.com). Other great resources for specialty ingredients are Burlap & Barrel (burlapandbarrel.com) and Penzeys (penzeys.com).

A Starter Guide to Hungarian Wine

by Athena Bochanis, wine importer and founder of Palinkerie

There is a powerful affinity between Hungarians and wine—because, of course, no Hungarian meal would be complete without it. Every person in Hungary, from the cashier at the deli to the customs agent at the airport, seems to be constantly sharing their opinion about wine, which just goes to show how universal it is.

Hungarian wine, like Hungarian food, is distinctly nostalgic. It evokes memories of centuries past, and every region has its legend and lore. Drinking the wines of Somló evokes a time when newlyweds believed that these fiery, salty wines would help them conceive a male heir. Sip Tokaji Aszú and you're transported to the tables of Peter the Great and Louis XIV. Hungarian wine is still overwhelmingly made in small batches by family-run wineries, which makes each vintage feel heartfelt and honest. You don't need to have Hungarian heritage to feel the connection to the past. The country's wine culture is more than a thousand years old, and that tradition pulsates in every bottle.

At the same time, Hungarian wine is evolving to meet a global marketplace. New wineries are constantly being founded; sons and daughters take over their parents' estates, committing to organic practices and wider distribution. Ancient native grapes like Csokaszőlő, Leányka, and Kadarka that were upstaged by international varieties in the 1990s have been rediscovered with a newfound appreciation. Hungarian wines are finding a place on the menus of Michelin-starred Korean, Indian, and Japanese restaurants in the United States. It is this ability to both carry on tradition and step into the future that makes Hungarian wine so special.

Hungary has twenty-two wine regions, spawning a wide range of styles and flavors. Opulent reds, herbal whites, volcanic wines, and sweet dessert styles that are light, medium, and full bodied: Hungary has them all. Broadly speaking, though, the wines are versatile and fun to pair with food. White wines are traditionally quite structured (from being left on the lees), red wines are on the drier end of the scale, and they both (generally) have great acidity. Below is an introduction to six of the major wine regions, along with their notable wines and grapes.

* Lake Balaton is a massive freshwater lake in western Hungary, surrounded by eight(!) different wine regions. It might seem like a lot, but the soil and climate change dramatically around the lake, depending on where you are and how far you are from

the water. You'll find mineral-rich terroir on the northern coastline, basalt volcanic soils on Somló and Badacsony, and a warmer climate in the south. Balaton is dazzlingly picturesque and a major holiday destination, and for that reason it is usually associated with fresh summery whites like Olaszrizling. However, volcanic wines (especially from Somló and Badacsony), fragrant whites like Tramini, and more recently natural wines (especially orange wines and pét-nats) are all worth seeking out. Today, Balaton is probably the most forward-thinking region in Hungary, and much of the burgeoning natural wine scene is concentrated here.

⭐ Eger and Mátra are neighboring regions northeast of Budapest. They are hilly with volcanic soil and a classic continental climate. Medium-plus reds are the main attraction (Kékfrankos, Kadarka, Pinot Noir), but elegant whites (like the native blend Egri Csillag, the Star of Eger) originate here too. Eger is world famous for its wines, especially the Egri Bikavér (Bull's Blood), a native red blend usually based on Kékfrankos. This long-standing recognition gives Eger an old-school vibe, with its rich wines made in classic styles. Mátra is the lesser-known region next door, but it shares a lot of Eger's volcanic terroir and comes at a lower price. Mátra is also somewhat of a hotbed for natural wine.

⭐ For warmer wines, head south to the regions of Villány and Szekszárd. The soil is mostly loess here, dotted with clay and limestone. Villány is the hotter of the two and is famous for its luscious full-bodied reds. It is particularly celebrated for Cabernet Franc, which has been hailed as having found a natural home in Villány. Szekszárd is north of Villány, and while quite a bit less famous—and less expensive—it is home to nicely structured rosés; medium- to full-bodied reds, including a Szekszárdi Bikavér; and Síller, a traditional dark-hued rosé style. Notable varieties include Kékfrankos, Kadarka, Cabernet Franc, and Cabernet Sauvignon.

⭐ The most recognized Hungarian region is Tokaj in the northeast corner of the country. It is home to the first vineyard classification system in the world and was the first demarcated wine region in the world, both enacted to ensure the integrity of its dessert wine, Tokaji Aszú. The climate is continental, and three rivers converge here, giving the region a long summer with notable humidity. These conditions are ideal for the development of botrytis, or noble rot. This harmless fungus creates tiny holes in the grape skins, concentrating the sugars in the grapes. This is what gives Tokaji Aszú (and other coveted Tokaji dessert wines) their legendary sweetness. But Tokaj shouldn't be synonymous with sweet; it produces stunning dry wines as well. For both dry and sweet wines, expect age-worthy structure and powerful flavors. The region's soil is intensely volcanic and mineral, and only six (white) varieties can be used in a Tokaji wine, most of them high in acid. Try the flagship variety Furmint for something more savory, and the lesser-known Hárslevelű for more waxy texture and honeyed aromatics.

Although Hungary's wine production isn't small (30 percent more than neighboring Austria, for example), the wines can be hard to find in stores in the United States. If you're ready to swirl a glass, places like Astor Wines and Spirits in New York (astorwines.com), Gramercy Wine and Spirits in New York (gramercywine.com), and Flatiron Wines in New York and San Francisco (flatiron-wines.com) carry a wide range of Hungarian wines and ship nationally. And remember, you can always ask your local store to stock more Hungarian wine.

As Hungarians say, Egészségedre! And to everyone else: Cheers!

A Quick Pronunciation Guide

Hungarian is a phonetic language, so words are generally pronounced as they are spelled. But to an English speaker, Hungarian can look like a brain teaser, with accents flying in every direction and consonant groupings that defy logic.

Like English, vowel sounds are more expansive than a simple *a*, *e*, *i*, *o*, and *u*. But Hungarian goes an extra step with accent marks to clue you in to the specific sound. When it comes to consonants, the *r* is rolled like in many European languages. Other consonant pairs might look strange on paper, but they're actually similar to sounds we make in English. And the most important rule is the easiest to remember: the emphasis always goes on the first syllable of each word.

Turn the page for a chart of the important sounds to know. Any letters not listed in the chart are consistent with typical English pronunciations.

A f<u>a</u>ther	**Á** <u>a</u>nimal	**C** ha<u>ts</u>	**CS** <u>ch</u>eese	**DZ** li<u>ds</u>	**DZS** <u>j</u>ar
E m<u>e</u>ss	**É** d<u>ay</u>	**GY** <u>d</u>oor	**I** s<u>i</u>t	**Í** s<u>ee</u>	**J** <u>y</u>ell
NY ca<u>ny</u>on	**O** b<u>o</u>at	**Ó** m<u>oo</u>n	**Ö** t<u>u</u>rn	**Ő** <u>eu</u>ro	**R** a rolled r
S <u>sh</u>ore	**SZ** <u>s</u>ign	**TY** bu<u>tch</u>er	**U** b<u>oo</u>t	**Ú** f<u>oo</u>d	**Ü** t<u>oo</u>
Ű s<u>i</u>r	**V** e<u>v</u>er	**Z** de<u>s</u>ert	**ZS** trea<u>s</u>ure		

Noshing is the official fourth meal of the Jewish diet, and snacking is just as innate to Hungarian culture too. An array of smaller bites is the perfect excuse to gather, eat, and gossip.

Noshing

If you'd told me the most famous dish to come out of my restaurant would be deviled eggs . . . well, it's surprising, but I'll take the distinction with pride. A deviled egg is so versatile, a kind of timeless budget food that feels fancy. Growing up, both of my grandmas always had hard-boiled eggs in the fridge for snacks and we ate them plain with salt. The problem was the eggs were boiled within an inch of their lives and there was nothing else to balance the intensely eggy flavor. This recipe is a perfect base, a jumping-off point for creativity, that sets the stage for a wide range of toppings and flavors.

Makes 1 dozen devils

Dressed Deviled Eggs

FOR THE MOUSSE

10 large eggs, boiled for 9 minutes, cooled and peeled (see "On Boiling Eggs")

¾ cup Japanese mayonnaise, such as Kewpie, or regular mayonnaise (preferably Hellmann's or Schmaltz Mayo, page 193)

2 teaspoons kosher salt

TO PLATE

6 large eggs, boiled for 8 minutes, cooled and peeled

Flaky sea salt and freshly ground black pepper

Good extra-virgin olive oil

Final touches

Sweet and sour pickles
Whole dill fronds
Chili crisp
White anchovy fillets
Fried chicken skin
Fish roe
Hot sauce

Make the mousse: Combine the 9-minute eggs, mayo, and kosher salt in a food processor and blend together until silky smooth, about 5 minutes, stopping to scrape down the sides of the bowl as necessary. Store the mousse in an airtight container in the refrigerator until ready to use or up to 1 day.

To plate: Unless you own a fancy deviled egg plate, the one with individual cubby holes, the eggs will have difficulty standing up on their own. I recommend dolloping 1 teaspoon of mousse underneath each egg to keep it stable on a large platter.

Cut the 8-minute eggs in half and leave the yolks in the center. Schmear about a tablespoon of mousse on each egg. Season with flaky salt and pepper and a drizzle of olive oil. From here, add any final touches you want!

Wine pairing: Try the deviled eggs with a sparkling rosé (pezsgő or pét-nat).

ON BOILING EGGS

Prepare an ice-water bath in a bowl large enough to comfortably fit your eggs. Bring a large pot of water to a boil over high heat. Use a spider strainer or a large slotted spoon to gently lower the eggs into the pot and immediately set a timer. Cooking for 6 minutes will yield a runny yolk, 8 minutes will be slightly gooey yolks, 9 minutes fully set. Transfer the eggs to an ice-water bath and soak for about 10 minutes, until cooled completely. Store the eggs in an airtight container in the refrigerator for up to 1 week. Before serving, peel and rinse under cold water to remove any small shell pieces.

My first run-in with chicken liver was at my bris, but I had more important things to worry about that day. When I was growing up, there was always the looming presence of chopped chicken livers in a crystal boat, surrounded by Carr's table water crackers and a bottle of Manischewitz wine, on Nana Arlene's table. Most of my early memories are of Papa Howie, Nana Arlene's husband, talking with liver breath, chewing loudly, and getting it all over his mouth. So understandably, I was terrified of liver well into my teens. But in adulthood, it's become a sort of obsession, and it's a centerpiece of the menu at Agi's Counter. My trick is adding cream cheese, an easy hack for more flavor and to boost the texture. Instead of mealy chopped liver, everything is pureed into one even, creamy mousse, and the tang of the cream cheese offsets the iron taste of the liver, while caramelized onions and port bring plenty of sweetness forward. It's so deliciously spreadable, it'll convert even the most fearful.

Makes 3 cups

Chicken Liver Mousse

Place the cleaned livers in a large bowl. Toss with a generous pinch of pink curing salt, if using, and let sit for up to 30 minutes. While the livers cure, start to caramelize the onions.

Heat the canola oil and butter in a large heavy-bottomed pot over medium-low heat until the butter is melted. Add the onions and 2 tablespoons of salt. Cook, stirring frequently with a wooden spoon to avoid burning, until the onions caramelize evenly, 20 to 25 minutes. Stir in the thyme and deglaze the pan with the port. Use the wooden spoon to scrape the bottom of the pot and release all the caramelized flavor that has formed at the bottom.

Once the port has almost completely boiled off, add the livers and stir. Cook the livers until they are medium-rare and rosy red, about 5 minutes. Remove the pot from the heat. Working in batches, transfer the livers and onions to a blender and blend with the cream cheese on high speed until mousse-like, 2 to 3 minutes. Set a fine-mesh sieve over a large bowl and use a rubber spatula to press the mixture through the sieve for an even, creamy texture. Between the curing salt and the salted onions, you likely won't have to season the mousse with even more salt, but it's always good to taste and adjust the seasoning to your liking.

Chill the mousse in an airtight container in the refrigerator for at least 2 hours and up to 24 hours before serving.

RECIPE CONTINUES

1 pound chicken livers, rinsed and drained

Pink curing salt (optional)*

3 tablespoons canola oil

2 tablespoons unsalted butter

2 medium yellow onions, thinly sliced

2 tablespoons kosher salt, plus more as needed

Leaves from 2 fresh thyme sprigs

⅓ cup ruby port or Merlot

12 ounces cream cheese (preferably Philadelphia), cut into cubes (1½ cups)

TO PLATE

Unsalted butter

4 thick slices Caraway Pullman (page 48) or any bread of your choosing

Flaky sea salt and freshly ground black pepper

Good extra-virgin olive oil

Cherry Caramel (page 204; optional)

Roughly chopped fresh dill (optional)

Thinly sliced shallots (optional)

To plate: Melt a few tablespoons of butter in a large skillet over medium-low heat. Add the bread (working in batches and adding more butter if needed) and griddle on each side until toasty and golden brown. Schmear the cold liver mousse over the bread. Garnish with flaky salt and pepper and a little olive oil. As a final touch, I like a sweet addition of cherry caramel or a savory finish with roughly chopped dill and thinly sliced shallot, but these additions are up to you.

Wine pairing: In Hungary, liver mousse is traditionally paired with a sweet Tokaji wine. Try this with a Tokaji late harvest, Tokaji Aszú, sweet Szamorodni, or similar.

*Salting is an optional step that keeps the livers from turning gray while cooking. If you don't have pink curing salt, just rinse and drain the livers before cooking.

ON CARAMELIZING ONIONS

Heavily salting the onions achieves two things: It draws out plenty of moisture to coat the bottom of the pot and prevent burning. It also releases all the natural sugars in the onions for an even caramel color all around. Stir frequently and be patient! It's crucial to take the time to develop a deep flavor in these onions.

A major part of the Jewish American diet is whitefish. When I was a kid in Boca Raton, Florida, our local deli, Bagel Works, had turquoise Formica counters, black and white cookies, stacks of Dr. Brown's sodas, and a massive case of whitefish salad dwarfing everything around it. We never left without a container of it to schmear on bagels or rye bread. In my early twenties, I worked at Prune, Chef Gabrielle Hamilton's East Village institution. She used to make a sable butter that blew my mind, bringing back a flood of Bagel Works memories. This recipe is inspired by her and the flavors I hold closest to my heart.

Makes 2 cups

Smoked Trout Butter

Combine the butter, flaked fish, and salt in a food processor and pulse 10 to 15 times, until thoroughly combined. Serve the butter right away or store in an airtight container in the refrigerator for up to 2 weeks. I recommend pulling the trout butter from the fridge about 1 hour before serving to soften. No one wants to schmear with cold, hard butter.

Wine pairing: This dish could work nicely with a Tokaji Furmint or Hárslevelű or with a similarly fuller-bodied, mineral-driven white.

4 sticks (1 pound) unsalted butter, softened

5 ounces smoked trout or whitefish, flaked

1½ teaspoons kosher salt

Pair with:
Country Club Crackers (page 46)
Cornmeal Blini (page 22)
or store-bought crackers

The base of this recipe comes from a Hungarian dish, körözött, a spiced cheese spread traditionally made with quark, kind of a chunkier cottage cheese. I grew up in Florida and spent the summers in North Carolina's Blue Ridge Mountains, so my love for Southern cooking is genuine and deep. In the summers, we ate a lot of pimento cheese, and I saw a bridge between these two very traditional Hungarian and American foods. (If that's not the origin story of my cooking, I don't know what is.) This dip pulls from both sides, with sweet paprika, caraway seeds, and raw onion mingling with a ton of sharp cheddar cheese. It's a perfect party dip or even better on toasted bread as a late-night sandwich after everyone leaves.

Makes 4 cups

Körözött (Hungarian Pimento Cheese)

16 ounces cream cheese (preferably Philadelphia), softened

1 cup piquillo peppers, drained and finely chopped

2 tablespoons Dijon mustard

1½ tablespoons fresh lemon juice

1 tablespoon kosher salt

1 tablespoon caraway seeds, toasted (see page 209)

1 tablespoon sweet Hungarian paprika

8 ounces sharp cheddar, shredded (2 cups)

½ large yellow onion, finely minced (½ cup)

TO PLATE

Minced chives

Freshly ground black pepper

Flaky sea salt

Chips, crackers, or toast

Combine the cream cheese, chopped peppers, mustard, lemon juice, kosher salt, caraway seeds, and paprika in a food processor and process for about 2 minutes, stopping to scrape down the sides of the bowl as needed, until you have a smooth mixture. Transfer to a large bowl and gently fold in the cheddar and onion until combined.

To plate: Scrape the körözött into a large serving bowl and garnish with chives, black pepper, and a pinch of flaky salt. Accompany with chips,* crackers, or toast.

Wine pairing: Try pairing körözött with a fuller-bodied white wine with greener flavors and aged in used oak, like Furmint, Zöldveltelini (Grüner Veltliner), or similar.

*Ruffles, if you have them.

I never really had blini growing up; my family is distinctly Hungarian, and blini were from just a little farther east in eastern Europe. Nana Arlene sometimes made dollar pancakes and dressed them up, but they weren't quite the same as that perfect little vessel, the blini. They're the ultimate muse, ready to be dressed up however you like, with a dash of shabby elegance, like a swanky 1970s living room party where everyone might be swingers. These blini are fortified with cornmeal for an extra-sturdy base and a pleasingly hearty texture. From there, the presentation is up to you. Arrange them on your finest serving platter or your most weathered cutting board. Dress them up with a precise baton of chive or a pearl spoonful of caviar, or go easy with a dollop of sour cream and a pinch of chopped herbs. They're perfect either way—just be hospitable and generous about it. I like to land somewhere in the middle of the high-low spectrum by serving the blini nice and hot with something acidic and cold to bring some zest to it. This peppery radish topping—a sort of quick faux-kraut—is the perfect refreshing touch, especially when paired with a zippy horseradish cream.

Makes 15 to 20 blini

Radish Kraut on Cornmeal Blini

FOR THE QUICK KRAUT
½ pound radishes,* cut into small batons

1 tablespoon kosher salt

FOR THE BLINI
1 cup all-purpose flour

1 cup finely ground yellow cornmeal

2 teaspoons baking powder

1 teaspoon kosher salt

½ teaspoon sugar

2 large eggs

⅔ cup buttermilk

⅓ cup sour cream

6 tablespoons unsalted butter, 4 tablespoons melted

Make the kraut: Combine the radishes and salt in a small bowl. Clean hands are the easiest tool for this next step. Squeeze and stir the radishes, really working the salt into them. Store the kraut in an airtight container in the refrigerator for at least 30 minutes or overnight.

Make the blini: Whisk together the flour, cornmeal, baking powder, salt, and sugar in a large bowl. In another large bowl, whisk the eggs, then whisk in the buttermilk, sour cream, the 4 tablespoons melted butter, and ⅓ cup water. Add the wet ingredients to the dry and whisk until combined and thick like a pancake batter. Cover the bowl with plastic wrap, or transfer to an airtight quart container, and refrigerate for at least 30 minutes or up to 1 week.

Melt the remaining 2 tablespoons butter in a large skillet over medium-high heat. Dollop the cornmeal batter by the tablespoon into mounds around the skillet (4 or 5 mounds per batch). Cook until the batter is puffy and golden brown on the bottom, 1 to 2 minutes. Use an offset spatula or small spatula to flip the blini, then cook on the other side until golden, 1 to 2 minutes. Transfer to a plate and continue to cook the remaining batter.**

*I suggest large radishes like watermelon or Purple Ninja.

**This uses all the batter, but you can make as many or as few as you want/need now and refrigerate the rest of the batter for later.

RECIPE CONTINUES

TO PLATE

Horseradish Cream (recipe follows)

Freshly ground black pepper

Fresh dill fronds

Smoked salmon roe (optional)

To plate: Arrange the blini on a serving tray. Dollop a teaspoon of horseradish cream in the center of each blini. Using a fork, garnish each blini with about a tablespoon of the radish kraut.* Finish with some pepper and dill fronds and, if using, roe.

Wine pairing: This dish pairs beautifully with a salty, savory Somlói white wine.

✖ *If your heart is saying more cream or more kraut, go for it!*

Makes 1½ cups

Horseradish Cream

1 cup sour cream

¼ cup crème fraîche

4 tablespoons prepared horseradish, drained

1 teaspoon fresh lemon juice

1 teaspoon freshly ground black pepper

Kosher salt, to taste

In a small bowl, whisk together all the ingredients with a big pinch of salt. Taste for seasoning, then cover tightly and store in the refrigerator for up to 2 days.

I have a very deep, intimate relationship with beets, including a beet tattoo on my arm. As a lifelong lover of pickles and everything acid, this recipe is in heavy rotation at the restaurant and in my home. The brine is simple—accented with the unusual addition of cinnamon, which adds a warm richness—and the pickles live in the fridge, so there's no need for a full canning process.

Makes 4 quarts

Pickled Beets

Toast the cloves in a large stainless-steel pot over medium heat, stirring occasionally, until very fragrant, about 4 minutes. Add 2½ cups water, the vinegar, and sugar. Increase the heat to high and bring to a boil.

Meanwhile, put the beets, bay leaves, garlic cloves, and cinnamon sticks in a 4-quart jar or several smaller containers. Ladle the hot liquid into the jar to cover the beets, then tightly seal. Let cool completely before storing in the refrigerator. The beets can be eaten after chilling for 2 hours, but are better the longer they sit. They will keep in the fridge for up to 2 months.

Wine pairing: The beets pair nicely with a fruitier white, like Sauvignon Blanc, and could also be fun with a skin-contact (orange) wine.

2 tablespoons whole cloves

2½ cups red wine vinegar

1¼ cups sugar

4 pounds red beets, boiled, peeled, and quartered (see "On Boiling Beets")

4 dried bay leaves

8 garlic cloves

2 cinnamon sticks

ON BOILING BEETS

Arrange the beets in a large pot or saucepan, then add water to cover and the juice of 1 lemon. (The acidity keeps the beets vibrant.) Bring to a boil over high heat, then reduce the heat to medium-low and simmer for 45 minutes to 1 hour, until a fork easily pierces the beets. Drain and rinse under cold water until cool enough to handle.

Pickled Beets (page 25),
Sweet & Sour Pickles (page 28),
and Pickled Cauliflower (page 29)

Some kids grow up with fruit punch mouth or ice cream hands; I grew up with pickle breath. Both of my grandmas had an endless supply of pickle jars. They would whack the lid on the counter and easily twist it off, their aged hands seeming like Superman's. Once they slid the jar my way, it was guaranteed that I would finish the whole thing in one sitting. And not just the pickles, I would drink the brine—with a spoon, for some reason, a very mannerly approach. This recipe is very nostalgic. With a heavily spiced brine that hits all the sweet, sour, and earthy notes I would ever want, it's pickle perfection. The smell alone is enough to transport me back to the kitchen table, watching Grandma Agi cook while my hand was buried deep in a jar.

Makes 2 quarts

Sweet & Sour Pickles

1 pound cucumbers (preferably Persian or Kirby), sliced into rounds

5 fresh dill fronds

3 garlic cloves, skin on, smashed

1½ teaspoons mustard seeds

1½ teaspoons coriander seeds

¾ teaspoon dill seeds

½ cup champagne vinegar

3 tablespoons sugar

1 tablespoon kosher salt

½ teaspoon ground turmeric

½ teaspoon crushed red pepper flakes

Layer the sliced cucumbers with the dill and smashed garlic in a 2-quart mason jar.

Place the mustard seeds, coriander seeds, and dill seeds in a large stainless-steel pot over medium heat and toast, stirring occasionally, until very fragrant, about 4 minutes. Add 1 cup water, the vinegar, sugar, salt, turmeric, and red pepper flakes. Increase the heat to high and bring to a boil.

Ladle the hot liquid into the jar to cover the cucumbers and tightly seal. Let cool completely before storing in the refrigerator. The pickles can be eaten after chilling for 24 hours but are better the longer they sit. They will keep in the fridge for up to 2 months.

Wine pairing: Pair the pickles with an aromatic, honeyed white wine, like a Hárslevelű or Rajnai Rizling.

For so long cauliflower was an unappreciated vegetable, usually limp and lifeless on the side of a plate. Now it's seen blasted under heat until charred and delicious or ground up into a carb-friendly "rice." But I've always preferred my cauliflower to be snappy, pickled, and straight out of the jar. This brine leans a little Italian, with red onion, dried oregano, and red wine vinegar, plus some earthy accents from coriander, cumin, and mustard seeds. It packs a punch of flavor but still highlights the nutty sweetness of one of my favorite vegetables.

Makes 2 quarts

Pickled Cauliflower

Layer the cauliflower and red onion in a 2-quart mason jar.

Place the coriander seeds, cumin seeds, and mustard seeds in a large stainless-steel pot over medium heat and toast, stirring occasionally, until very fragrant, about 4 minutes. Add 3 cups water, the vinegar, garlic cloves, sugar, salt, and dried oregano. Increase the heat to high and bring to a boil.

Ladle the hot liquid into the jar to cover the cauliflower and tightly seal. Let cool completely before storing in the refrigerator. The cauliflower can be eaten after chilling for 48 hours but is better the longer it sits. Store the cauliflower in the refrigerator for up to 2 months.

Wine pairing: Pickled foods like this dish pair nicely with more fruit-forward whites; try Egri Csillag, unoaked Hárslevelű, or even a skin-contact (orange) wine.

*If you're shopping the farmers' market, swap the cauliflower for its jagged sister, Romanesco, or any of the colorful varieties.

1 large head of cauliflower,* cut into florets

½ small red onion, thinly sliced

1 tablespoon coriander seeds

1 teaspoon cumin seeds

1 teaspoon yellow mustard seeds

1¼ cups red wine vinegar

2 garlic cloves, skin on, smashed

3 tablespoons plus 1 teaspoon sugar

2 tablespoons plus 1 teaspoon kosher salt

2 tablespoons dried oregano

I have a love for almonds of all kinds, especially the wasabi-flavored ones. One of my most specific childhood memories was going to Nana Arlene's or Grandma Agi's house and being greeted by a full spread of noshes. There was usually a chaotic mix of bowls of M&M's, Ferrero Rocher, almonds, cashews, and, of course, chopped liver. But there were always bowls of super-salty nuts, which is where I planted myself. This version uses a paprika from Hungary, Espelette, that's really rich and deep in flavor, plus lots of salt with smoked paprika and nutritional yeast for umami. They're the perfect nosh for a glass of wine, a can of beer, and a circle of friends, with "Cheeto-dust" fingers to lick after.

Makes 3 cups

Fried Almonds & Paprika Salt

Make the paprika salt: Whisk together the salt, nutritional yeast, smoked paprika, and Espelette in a small bowl.

Make the almonds: Line a large plate or small baking sheet with paper towels.

Heat the olive oil in a large skillet over medium heat. The oil should be shimmering hot but not yet smoking. Carefully add the almonds to the oil. Stirring frequently with a wooden spoon, fry for 5 to 7 minutes, until the almonds are toasted and very fragrant. Use a spider strainer or large slotted spoon to transfer the almonds to the paper towels to drain. Season immediately with the paprika salt. Let cool before serving, but I do enjoy these while still warm. Store any leftovers for up to 3 days in an airtight container with paper towels lining the bottom.

Wine pairing: This dish goes perfectly with Olaszrizling or another medium-bodied white with savory flavors.

FOR THE PAPRIKA SALT

1 tablespoon kosher salt

1 tablespoon nutritional yeast

1 teaspoon smoked paprika

1 teaspoon Espelette powder or flakes

FOR THE ALMONDS

½ cup extra-virgin olive oil

3 cups raw almonds, skin on

Lecsó, comprising marinated charred peppers, is one of those dishes in Hungary that's extremely versatile (every family uses it differently) and extremely controversial (every family looks down on everyone else's). It can be the base of a dish, the base of a sauce, served on the side as a condiment, or eaten as the full dish itself. My version is served as a nosh, with a mix of bell and Anaheim peppers, but grab whatever peppers look good at the grocery or are in season at the market. Just make sure to char them well for a deep smoky flavor. Serve with crackers for ribboning the marinated peppers or a pile of warm bread to sop up the juice—it's a simple and satisfying bite either way. The flavors only improve the longer it sits—like leftover pizza, it's better the day after—so make it ahead and bring to room temperature an hour before serving.

Makes 4 cups

Lecsó (Marinated Blistered Peppers)

Begin by charring the bell and Anaheim peppers over an open flame. This can be done over a gas stovetop or a grill on high heat. Use tongs to hold the peppers over the flame, rotating until blackened on all sides but not ashy. Transfer the peppers to a medium bowl, wrap tightly with plastic wrap, and let rest for 30 minutes. This will make peeling the skins off easier.

Unwrap the peppers. They should be deflated and droopy. Gently tear the stem and core out of each pepper and discard. If some seeds scatter, that's OK! Use your fingers to peel the blackened skins off the peppers and discard.*

Place the peeled peppers in a separate medium bowl and tear them into rustic strips, about 1 inch thick. Add the onion, garlic, salt, cumin, olive oil, and vinegar. Toss until thoroughly combined. Let the mixture marinate for at least 2 hours before serving, but this is best made 1 day ahead.

When ready to serve, lay the peppers flat on a serving platter, then top them with the onion and its juices. Serve with crackers or warm bread.

Wine pairing: Pair this dish with a bright red, like Kadarka, or the traditional Síller, a dark-hued rosé.

3 red bell peppers

2 Anaheim peppers

½ medium yellow onion, thinly sliced

1 garlic clove, grated or minced

1 teaspoon kosher salt

½ teaspoon ground cumin

⅔ cup extra-virgin olive oil

2 tablespoons red wine vinegar

Country Club Crackers (page 46) or crusty warm bread

*The char will break up and mingle with the pepper "tears," which creates valuable flavor, so no need to be perfect here.

Grandma Agi didn't make lecsó very often, but every time I went to Hungary, she demanded I bring back the lecsó-flavored Maggi cubes, which she often used as the base of her cooking.

This recipe is pure Nana Arlene. Every Sunday we'd gather at her house, grabbing a bunch of stuff from Bagel Works on the way, like a tub of whitefish, a stack of cured lox, and a pile of bagels. This recipe is an easy curing process that takes a few pantry ingredients and very little effort, and it can be started on Friday to be ready by Sunday. When it comes to slicing, I recommend a very, very sharp knife that will glide through the salmon flesh for paper-thin pieces. I like to serve it simply, surrounded by crackers and covered in herbs. Or go for abundance on a big board with bread, dips, spreads, pickles, basically this entire chapter circling around it. It's a perfect vibrant pink centerpiece to pick at slowly, mix and match, and nosh all day.

Makes 3 pounds of cured salmon

Dill & Fennel Seed Cured Salmon

1 (3-pound) center-cut salmon fillet

½ cup kosher salt

½ cup sugar

2 tablespoons fennel seeds, toasted (see page 209)

2 tablespoons black peppercorns

1 large bunch of fresh dill

TO PLATE

Flaky sea salt and freshly ground black pepper

Good extra-virgin olive oil

Fresh herbs, such as chives, tarragon, or parsley

Edible blossoms (optional)

Halved lemon

Crackers

Set the salmon, skin side down, on a cutting board and cut the fillet crosswise into 2 pieces. Stir together the kosher salt, sugar, fennel seeds, and black peppercorns in a small bowl. Evenly sprinkle both fillets with the spice mixture. Fan out the dill on 1 fillet so it covers the flesh. Place the other fillet on top to make a salmon and dill sandwich.

Wrap the salmon tightly in plastic wrap. Place in a baking dish or roasting pan. Cover with aluminum foil. Set a second baking dish (the same size or smaller) on top, weigh it down with heavy cans, and refrigerate for 2 days or up to 2 weeks.

To plate: Remove the salmon from the fridge and unwrap. Separate the fillets, discard the dill, and scrape off any excess salt mixture. With a sharp carving knife, thinly slice the salmon and arrange on a large serving tray. Garnish the tray with flaky salt and pepper, olive oil, fresh herbs, and (if using) edible blossoms. In the spring and summer, when herb blossoms are most bountiful, I love to throw tarragon leaves, brassica flowers, arugula flowers, and chive blossoms on here! Serve with lemon halves and crackers.

Wine pairing: This dish pairs beautifully with sparkling white wine or with a rosé (try rosé made from Kékfrankos or a Kékfrankos blend).

Agi used to make this simple nosh all the time, grabbing a few things from the fridge—a block of butter, some stray dill, the cheap caviar that she got from the grocery store—and toasting slices of rye bread. It was nothing fancy, but it really hit the spot as a quick snack or small meal, like pouring a bowl of cereal in the afternoon or for dinner. It's a small treat I've adopted in my own kitchen because it's so simple to make and hits all the pleasure centers of salty, buttery, briny, and herby. This is one of those recipes that's best assembled without measurements. Follow your heart and use as much as you'd like or as little. Although I say, the more butter and roe, the better!

Serves 1

Caraway Toast & Roe

Caraway Pullman (page 48), sliced thick, or slices of store-bought rye bread

Unsalted butter, room temperature

Smoked trout roe

Fresh dill, roughly chopped

Flaky sea salt, crushed

Toast the bread in a large nonstick skillet over medium heat with a decent amount of butter. Press down on the bread occasionally to ensure even toasting. It's important the bread be golden brown and crackling with butter. Repeat on the other side. Remove from the pan and transfer to a plate. While hot, schmear more butter on the bread followed by big clusters of smoked trout roe, a generous sprinkling of dill, and a pinch of crushed flaky salt. Eat immediately and repeat the process as many times as you need.

Wine pairing: This pairs perfectly with a lively aromatic white wine, like Cserszegi Fűszeres or Egri Csillag.

My grandmothers taught me that a meal isn't complete without a carb on the table. This chapter mixes faithful classics with updates on the traditions, plus my favorite way to use each one.

Breads, Biscuits & Crackers

Pogácsa are iconic Hungarian biscuits, usually fairly small and meant to be served alongside a meal or with jam and butter. Sometimes they're studded with cheese, sometimes pork rinds, sometimes both. This version was designed for Agi's Counter by our original pastry chef, Renee Hudson. They're generously sized and packed with cheddar and dill (it wouldn't be Agi's Counter without dill). I remember going to Hungary for the first time and knowing in my soul that pogácsa was meant for a breakfast sandwich. Below is my spin on a bodega egg and cheese sandwich, using my favorite carb as the vessel.

Makes 30 biscuits

Pogácsa (Dill & Cheddar Biscuits)

Whisk together the warm milk, yeast, and sugar in a small bowl. Let stand for about 5 minutes until foamy and fragrant. In a separate small bowl, whisk together the eggs and sour cream. In the bowl of a stand mixer fitted with the paddle attachment, mix the flour, cheddar, dill, butter, and salt on low speed until combined. Add the yeast mixture and egg mixture to the bowl with the flour mixture. Mix on medium speed until everything is fully incorporated into a tacky dough, about 3 minutes. Use a rubber spatula to scrape the sides and bottom of the bowl.

Cut two 32-inch-long pieces of parchment and lay them on a work surface. Spray both pieces with nonstick cooking spray. Transfer the dough to one piece of parchment. Lay the other piece of parchment on top, greased side down, and use a rolling pin to roll the dough to the edges. Peel off the top parchment and use a bench scraper or metal spatula to lift the dough and fold it into thirds, like a letter. Place the second piece of parchment back on top and roll the dough to the edges again. Repeat the folding and rolling process 2 more times, for a total of 3 foldings.

The final rolled dough should be about 1 inch thick. Slide the parchment onto a rimmed baking sheet and place in the freezer for 20 to 30 minutes, until the dough is very stiff. Use a sharp knife to make hatch marks across the entire surface of the dough. Use a 3-inch round cookie or biscuit cutter to cut 30 biscuits from the dough. Discard the scraps or bake them off separately. Transfer the biscuits to two clean large rimmed baking sheets lined with parchment. Cover

½ cup whole milk, slightly warm

1¾ teaspoons active dry yeast

1 teaspoon sugar

2 large eggs

½ cup sour cream

3¼ cups plus 2 tablespoons all-purpose flour

5 ounces aged cheddar, grated (1¼ cups)

1½ cups chopped fresh dill

14 tablespoons unsalted butter, cubed

2 tablespoons kosher salt

Nonstick cooking spray

RECIPE CONTINUES

loosely with plastic wrap and set somewhere warm to proof until doubled in size, 1½ to 2 hours. (Near the oven is always a good spot to get ambient heat.)

Preheat the oven to 325°F.

Remove the plastic wrap and bake the biscuits for 20 minutes, rotating halfway through, until golden brown and fluffy. Transfer to a wire rack to cool before serving. Honestly, I can never wait so I usually rip one open while it's still piping hot and schmear it with salted butter. Any leftover biscuits can be wrapped and refrigerated for up to 1 week or frozen for up to 1 month.

Serves 4

Pogácsa Morning Fried Egg Biscuit

Unsalted butter, for the skillet

4 Pogácsa (page 41), sliced in half horizontally

4 large eggs

½ cup mayonnaise

8 ounces sharp white cheddar

Melt a good knob of butter in a large skillet over low heat. Toast the cut sides of the pogácsa until golden brown, about 4 minutes. If working in batches, add more butter to the pan as needed. You can set your oven to 250°F to keep your biscuits warm while you prepare the rest.

Once you've toasted all your pogácsa, cook the eggs. Keep a clean plate nearby. Wipe out the skillet, add more butter, and melt it over medium-high heat. Crack 2 eggs into the skillet and fry in the butter until the sides begin to crisp, about 3 minutes. Use a spatula to flip the eggs and fry on the other side for about 30 seconds. You want the egg to still be soft. Transfer to the plate and repeat with the remaining 2 eggs.

To assemble, spread 1 tablespoon of mayo on each biscuit half. It should be a thin layer. Add 1 egg to each bottom half of the biscuit. Using a Microplane or grater, shred a nice high pile of cheese on top of each egg. Cover with the remaining biscuit half and serve immediately.

Lángos is a street food, the Hungarian version of fried dough. It's sold across the country, usually from a little stand, fried to order, coming out like big barren pizza disks. I've been to Hungary in the winter when it was so bitterly cold, and getting a piping hot lángos wrapped in oil-soaked parchment was the best thing. This version is pretty faithful to the original, except for the garnishes. When I was the executive chef at the Eddy, I served a savory lángos with garlic honey and cheese and it became super popular. But I also like leaning sweet with rhubarb jam and walnuts. Sweet or salty doesn't matter; my only advice is to make as many as possible.

Makes 12 small lángos

Lángos (Fried Bread)

Place the potatoes in a large pot and cover with cold water. Bring to a boil over high heat and cook until fork-tender, 15 to 20 minutes. Drain thoroughly and cool slightly. The potato will become harder to work with if it gets too cool. Use a ricer or food mill to process the potatoes into a large bowl or use a potato masher.

Whisk together the warm milk, olive oil, yeast, and sugar in a small bowl. Let stand for about 5 minutes until foamy and fragrant. Add the flour and kosher salt to the bowl with the potatoes. Rub the mixture through your hands to incorporate the flour and make small pebbles. Add the yeast mixture to the potato-flour mixture and use a wooden spoon to mix until a wet, cohesive dough forms. Cover loosely with plastic wrap and set somewhere warm to proof until doubled in size, about 1½ hours. (Near the oven is always a good spot to get ambient heat.)

Lightly flour a work surface and your hands. Tear a golf ball–size amount of dough and press it on the work surface using your fingertips. You should have a flat disk with dimples in it. Don't press too hard and don't make it too flat. Continue with the remaining dough to make 12 disks. Arrange the disks on a baking sheet lined with parchment paper if you need more room.

Line a large plate or small baking sheet with paper towels. Heat the canola oil to 350°F in a large Dutch oven over medium heat. Lower 3 or 4 lángos into the oil, being careful not to overcrowd, and fry for 1 minute per side until golden brown and puffy. Remove from the oil using a slotted spoon or spider strainer and set on the paper towels to drain. Sprinkle with flaky salt while the lángos are still hot. Continue frying the rest of the dough and serve warm.

2 medium Yukon Gold potatoes, peeled and diced into 1-inch pieces

1 cup whole milk, slightly warm

3 tablespoons extra-virgin olive oil

1 tablespoon active dry yeast

2 teaspoons sugar

3 cups 00 flour,* plus more for the work surface

1½ teaspoons kosher salt

Canola oil, for frying (about 2 quarts, depending on the size of your pot)

Flaky sea salt

*You can substitute all-purpose flour if you want, but the lángos are more pillowy with 00.

RECIPE CONTINUES

VARIATIONS

Savory Lángos

Serves 6 to 12

12 piping hot Lángos
(Fried Bread; page 43)

1½ cups Fermented Garlic
Honey (page 195)

9 ounces pecorino cheese,
grated (2¼ cups)

While each lángos is still hot, drizzle 2 tablespoons of garlic honey over the entire surface, then top with 3 tablespoons of cheese. Serve immediately.

Sweet Lángos

Serves 6 to 12

12 piping hot Lángos
(Fried Bread; page 43)

1½ cups cinnamon sugar

Plum Compote (page 207)

While each lángos is still hot, sprinkle 2 tablespoons of cinnamon sugar over the surface. Serve immediately with plenty of plum compote for spreading.

Nana Arlene always belonged to a country club, and when I was little, she would bring me along to enjoy the omelet station and ice sculptures. I can remember her so distinctly in her collared sweater, with a plate of salted tomatoes, cured salmon, and these absolutely massive crackers. She has always been extra petite, so the scale of the crackers was comically large. But she would methodically spread some butter, arrange the fish and tomato, and work her way through. (At Agi's Counter, the Country Club plate is in Nana Arlene's honor.) These crackers are modeled after a sort of lavash cracker, big and bubbly. And the cracker sandwich, made with smoked whitefish and plenty of dill, is perfect for invoking your own inner Nana Arlene.

Makes six 8-inch crackers

Country Club Crackers

⅔ cup warm water (around 100°F)

2¼ teaspoons active dry yeast (from a ¼-ounce packet)

1 teaspoon honey

1½ cups all-purpose flour

½ cup rye flour

1 tablespoon extra-virgin olive oil, plus more for the bowl

2 teaspoons kosher salt

1 large egg white, beaten

Flaky sea salt

Combine ⅓ cup of the warm water with the yeast and honey in a food processor. Let stand for about 5 minutes until foamy and fragrant. Add the remaining ⅓ cup water, then the all-purpose flour, rye flour, olive oil, and kosher salt. Pulse the dough until a soft dough ball forms around the blade. Transfer the ball of dough to a large bowl, lightly greased with olive oil. Cover and let rise for 45 to 50 minutes.

Preheat the oven to 400°F and set a rack in the center. Line a rimmed baking sheet with parchment paper.

Turn out the dough and divide it into 6 equal balls. Roll 1 ball of dough into a roughly 8-inch round. It's OK if the shape isn't perfect—these crackers have a posh name, but they're rustic in spirit. Place the rolled dough on one side of the prepared baking sheet. Repeat with a second piece of dough, setting it on the other side of the baking sheet. Brush each cracker with the beaten egg white and sprinkle flaky salt over the dough, crushing it between your fingers as you do.

Bake for about 12 minutes, turning the baking sheet halfway through, until the crackers are golden brown and crisp. Slide them onto a wire rack to cool completely. Repeat with the remaining dough, letting the baking sheet cool slightly between each batch.

Once the crackers have cooled completely, break them into large pieces. Serve immediately or store in a plastic zip-top bag at room temperature for up to 5 days.

Smoked Whitefish Salad & Cracker Sandwich

Mix together the fish, sour cream, onion, mustard, dill, lemon zest and juice, and salt and pepper to taste in a large bowl.

To plate: Spread about 1 cup of salad onto a cracker. Sprinkle generously with chopped dill. Top the salad with another cracker. Break into large pieces and serve.

1 pound smoked whitefish or smoked trout, bones removed and flaked

1 cup sour cream

2 tablespoons finely chopped red onion

1 teaspoon Dijon mustard

¼ cup chopped fresh dill

Zest and juice of 1 lemon

Kosher salt and freshly ground black pepper

TO PLATE

6 Country Club Crackers (opposite), unbroken

Chopped fresh dill

My childhood was filled with Jewish deli and diner sandwiches, always on caraway-studded rye bread or simple slices of white bread. This pullman loaf is a combo of both—my perfect sandwich bread—an extra fluffy white bread with strong notes of caraway. I like to make it in a 13-inch loaf pan for one big loaf, but this dough can also be divided between two 8 × 4-inch pans. And what good is sandwich bread without sandwiches? The tuna melt is one of the most popular items on the Agi's Counter menu and a personal favorite of mine. And my ultimate version of a turkey club is in honor of my dad, who has always said, "You can tell how good a diner is by their turkey club."

Makes 1 loaf

Caraway Pullman

2 teaspoons active dry yeast

1 cup warm water (around 100°F)

⅔ cup whole milk

6 tablespoons unsalted butter, room temperature

2¼ teaspoons kosher salt

4¾ cups all-purpose flour, plus more for the work surface

¼ cup full-fat milk powder

3 tablespoons caraway seeds

3 tablespoons sugar

3 tablespoons potato starch

Nonstick cooking spray

In the bowl of a stand mixer fitted with the hook attachment, combine the yeast and warm water. Let stand for about 5 minutes, until foamy and fragrant. Add the milk, butter, salt, flour, milk powder, caraway seeds, sugar, and potato starch and knead the dough on medium speed until smooth, elastic, and pulling away from the sides, about 10 minutes. (Alternatively, you can mix and knead by hand until a smooth ball of dough has formed.) Loosely cover the bowl with plastic wrap and set somewhere warm to proof until doubled in size, 1½ to 2 hours. (Near the oven is always a good spot to get ambient heat.)

Spray a 13-inch loaf pan with nonstick cooking spray. Lightly flour a work surface and turn out the dough. Use your hands to roll and shape the dough into a 13-inch log, then transfer to the prepared loaf pan. Loosely cover the pan with plastic wrap and set somewhere warm to proof until doubled in size, 45 minutes to 1 hour.

About 15 minutes before baking, preheat the oven to 350°F.

Remove the plastic wrap from the loaf pan and bake the loaf for 30 to 40 minutes, until evenly golden brown or the bread reaches an internal temperature of 190°F. Remove from the oven and invert onto a cooling rack. Cool completely before slicing. Any leftover bread can be wrapped and refrigerated for up to 1 week or frozen for up to 1 month.

Turkey Club (page 51) and
Confit Tuna Melt (page 50)

Confit Tuna Melt

1 (3- to 4-pound) Albacore tuna center-cut loin, bloodline and skin removed

Kosher salt

8 cups extra-virgin olive oil

1 garlic head, cut in half horizontally

2 dried bay leaves

4 celery stalks, thinly sliced

1 cup chopped fresh dill

½ cup thinly sliced pickled peppers

1½ cups mayonnaise

¼ cup Dijon mustard

TO ASSEMBLE

12 slices (½ inch thick) Caraway Pullman (page 48)

Mayonnaise or Schmaltz Mayo (page 193)

8 ounces sharp cheddar, grated (2 cups)

Unsalted butter, room temperature

Preheat the oven to 350°F.

Pat the tuna dry with paper towels and season both sides with plenty of salt. Place in a 9 × 13-inch baking dish and cover with the olive oil. The tuna should be completely submerged. Nestle in the garlic halves and bay leaves. Cover the dish tightly with aluminum foil and bake for about 1 hour. The tuna should easily flake apart when touched. Let cool completely in the oil. This can be done a day ahead—just transfer the covered baking dish to the refrigerator until ready to use.

If using right away, leave the oven on, still set at 350°F. Set a wire rack in a rimmed baking sheet and place it in the oven to preheat.

When the tuna is cool enough to handle, transfer to a large bowl. Strain the olive oil and freeze it for dressing for a seafood salad, roasting fish, finishing salads, or building flavor in sauces. Use a fork to flake the tuna until it's all broken up. Add the celery, dill, peppers, mayo, and mustard. Toss until thoroughly combined.

To assemble: Lay 6 bread slices on a work surface. Schmear each slice with a thin coating of mayo. Thin! Don't go crazy. Sprinkle the grated cheese over each slice of bread and gently press into the mayo so it sticks. Scoop about ½ cup of tuna salad on each slice and press into the cheese a little. Top with the remaining slices of bread.

Melt a generous amount of butter, about 3 heaping tablespoons, in a large nonstick skillet over medium heat. Working in batches, toast 1 or 2 sandwiches (depending what fits in your skillet) for 3 to 4 minutes on each side, pressing down with a spatula from time to time, until golden brown. Transfer to the wire rack in the oven for about 5 minutes, until the cheese begins to ooze out the sides. Meanwhile, continue frying the remaining sandwiches, adding more butter as needed. Cut each sandwich in half on the diagonal before serving.

Turkey Club

Line a plate with paper towels. Working in batches, sear the bacon in a large skillet over medium-high heat, flipping halfway, until golden brown and crispy, 6 to 8 minutes. Transfer to the paper towels to drain. Drain the bacon fat and reserve for another use.

Return the skillet to medium heat. Melt a large knob of butter, then add the bread in batches and toast on both sides until golden brown, about 4 minutes on each side. Lay the slices flat on a large baking sheet. Once all the bread is toasted, schmear 1 tablespoon of the mayo on each slice.

There's some controversy on how to layer a club sandwich. Whatever, this is how I layer: Place 1 leaf of lettuce on the bottom slice of bread. Top with 1 slice of tomato, followed by 4 slices of folded turkey. Finish with 2 slices of bacon and the remaining bread. I like to insert two toothpicks to hold the sandwich together and then cut them in half between the toothpicks.

My opinion is club sandwiches are best served with slaw, pickles, and a root beer.

8 slices (½ inch thick) Cured Bacon (page 200) or store-bought bacon

Unsalted butter, for the skillet

8 slices (½ inch thick) Caraway Pullman (page 48)

½ cup Schmaltz Mayo (page 193) or store-bought mayonnaise

4 large leaves gem lettuce, butter lettuce, or romaine

1 large ripe, juicy tomato, thinly sliced

1 pound store-bought smoked turkey breast

Growing up, I ate dozens of pounds of challah. It kicked off every Friday at my Jewish day school, and then it was at the center of the table for every shabbat and holiday. There's a tradition at the end of bar or bat mitzvahs and weddings where everyone tears off pieces from a large loaf of challah. I always loved that moment. It felt so communal and comforting to me, like everyone was braided into the bread. So I wanted to make a challah that was, excuse my language, really fucking huge. Big enough for a twenty-person dinner, big enough to freeze and use over and over, and big enough to make 2 loaves to get you through shabbat. My favorite challahs are always super yellow and eggy, and I think a sprinkle of sesame seeds on top looks like little stars across the dark surface. And speaking of eggy, challah and French toast are a match made in heaven. I love really thick slices, stacked, and covered in fruit compote with plenty of maple syrup.

Makes 1 huge challah or 2 smaller loaves

Sesame Challah

2¼ teaspoons active dry yeast (from a ¼-ounce packet)

2 teaspoons plus ¾ cup sugar

2¼ cups warm water (around 100°F)

1 stick (8 tablespoons) unsalted butter, melted

2 large eggs, beaten

5 teaspoons kosher salt

7 cups all-purpose flour

2 tablespoons extra-virgin olive oil

2 large egg yolks

Sesame seeds*

*I also like to make this with flaxseeds and/or poppy seeds.

Whisk together the yeast, 2 teaspoons of the sugar, and ¼ cup of the warm water in a small bowl. Let stand for about 5 minutes until foamy and fragrant. In the bowl of a stand mixer fitted with the whisk attachment, beat the butter, eggs, salt, the remaining ¾ cup sugar, and the remaining 2 cups warm water on low speed until combined. Add the flour and the yeast mixture. Switch to the hook attachment and knead the dough on medium speed until smooth, elastic, and pulling away from the sides, about 10 minutes.

Rub a large bowl with the olive oil. Transfer the dough to the bowl, cover loosely with plastic wrap, and set somewhere warm to proof until doubled in size, 1½ to 2 hours. (Near the oven is always a good spot to get ambient heat.) Uncover the dough and lightly punch it down. At this point, you can decide to make 2 normal-size loaves or 1 large-ass loaf of challah. If making 2 loaves, divide the dough into 6 even pieces. If making 1 loaf, divide into 3 pieces.

Regardless of how many you make, the braiding works the same here. On a clean surface, use your hands to roll the divided dough into roughly 17-inch-long strands. Don't worry about them being perfect. I think irregularly shaped bread is beautiful. Place 1 dough strand in the center. Pinch the other 2 strands onto one end of the center strand, creating somewhat of an open triangle. Braid the 3 strands, going over and under the middle strand until you run out of dough. Twist the ends

RECIPE CONTINUES

of the challah into itself to create a braided ball and pinch the seams together. Repeat with the remaining dough, if making 2 loaves.

Transfer to a large rimmed baking sheet lined with parchment paper (or two baking sheets) and cover loosely with plastic wrap. Set somewhere warm to proof until doubled in size, 30 minutes to 1 hour.

About 15 minutes before baking, preheat the oven to 325°F.

While the oven preheats, whisk the egg yolks with 2 tablespoons of water. Uncover the challah and brush with the egg yolk mixture. Sprinkle a generous amount of sesame seeds over the challah. Bake for 15 minutes. Increase the temperature to 425°F and rotate the baking sheet. Continue to bake for 20 to 25 minutes for 1 large loaf, or about 15 minutes for 2 small loaves. I enjoy a deep-colored challah, so this recipe will produce a much darker bread. Don't be alarmed! Transfer the challah to a wire rack and let cool completely before cutting into it. Any leftover challah can be wrapped and stored at room temperature for a week.

Serves 4

Challah French Toast

FOR THE FRENCH TOAST

6 large eggs

1½ cups half-and-half

1 teaspoon orange zest

1 teaspoon kosher salt

1 tablespoon unsalted butter, plus more for the skillet

Sesame Challah (page 52), sliced 2 inches thick

TO PLATE

Unsalted butter

Pure maple syrup

Blueberry Coriander Compote (page 206) or any fruit jam

Confectioners' sugar

Preheat the oven to 250°F. Set a wire rack in a rimmed baking sheet and place in the oven to preheat.

Whisk together the eggs, half-and-half, orange zest, and salt in a 9 × 13-inch baking dish. Heat 1 tablespoon of butter in a large skillet over medium-low heat. Working in batches, soak a few challah slices in the egg mixture for about 1 minute on each side. Transfer to the skillet and fry for about 2 minutes on each side until golden brown. Transfer to the wire rack in the oven to keep warm while you soak and fry the remaining slices. Add more butter to the skillet as needed.

For a dramatic plating, schmear butter on each slice of toast. Stack all the slices on top of each other on a very large serving plate. Drizzle generously with maple syrup, spoon the compote over top, and dust with confectioners' sugar.

Soups are the heart and soul of Hungarian cuisine.
They range from healing to celebratory,
casual to elegant, winter to summer.
Every moment is the right moment for soup.

Soups

One of the most popular soups at Agi's Counter is this cold, refreshing borscht. It's a little sweet, a little acidic, a little creamy, and so cooling in the humid summer. It reminds me of a borscht I used to get with Nana Arlene at the Jewish deli in Florida, which felt like a prize after wading through the swampy weather. In this version, I round out the flavors a little with shallots and bay leaves. Red wine vinegar is the classic pairing, but I really love the herbal notes of my homemade Chamomile Vinegar (page 194) if you have a batch lying around. Just make sure to freeze the serving glasses an hour before serving, then go outside to enjoy in the hot weather.

Serves 4

Chilled Buttermilk Borscht

2 pounds red beets, peeled and halved

2 large shallots, sliced

2 garlic cloves, smashed

2 dried bay leaves

4 teaspoons red wine vinegar or Chamomile Vinegar (page 194), plus more as needed

1 tablespoon sugar

1 tablespoon extra-virgin olive oil

Kosher salt

1 cup full-fat buttermilk*

*Use really good quality, such as Five Acre Farms or Ronnybrook

TO PLATE

Pickled Grapes (page 205)

Fennel seeds, toasted and ground (see page 209)

Extra-virgin olive oil

Combine the beets, shallots, garlic, bay leaves, vinegar, sugar, olive oil, and a big pinch of salt in a large pot. Cover with about 12 cups water to completely submerge everything. Bring to a boil, then reduce to a low simmer and cook for 30 to 45 minutes, until the beets are fork-tender. Fish out the bay leaves. Transfer everything else to a blender and blend until smooth. Taste for seasoning, adding salt and vinegar as needed. It should be slightly tart and vibrant. Let cool completely before whisking in the buttermilk. Chill for 30 minutes or up to 1 hour before serving.

To plate: Ladle the borscht into tall drinking glasses. Each portion should receive a pickled grape, dusting of ground fennel seeds, and drizzle of olive oil.

Wine pairing: Pair the borscht with Kékfrankos rosé or with a medium-bodied unoaked dry white (Olaszrizling, Szürkebarát, Furmint, or similar) from Eger, Mátra, or Lake Balaton.

Chilled Sorrel Soup (page 60),
Chilled Buttermilk Borscht (page 58),
Meggyleves (page 61)

Sorrel, a staple of eastern European cooking, is a leafy green herb known for its distinctive lemony taste (not to be confused with Caribbean sorrel, another name for hibiscus). It pops up at farmers' markets or in CSA boxes in spring and summer and this soup is a light and satisfying way to use it in abundance. The tartness of sorrel finds a great balance with the richness of heavy cream and the body of a starchy potato. Just make sure to add the sorrel at the very end so the leaves stay vibrantly green. This can be served warm, but I think the sorrel is more punchy and refreshing when it's had time to chill and fully infuse the soup.

Serves 4

Chilled Sorrel Soup

9 tablespoons unsalted butter, cold

1 large shallot, thinly sliced

1 small russet potato, scrubbed and diced into small pieces

2 cups vegetable stock

3 cups green sorrel (about 10 ounces)

½ cup heavy cream

Kosher salt

Melt 8 tablespoons of the butter in a small saucepan over medium heat. Add the shallot and potato. Cook, stirring occasionally, until the shallot is translucent, about 5 minutes. Add the stock and bring to a simmer. Cook for about 10 minutes, until the potato is fork-tender. Transfer to a blender and blend until smooth. Add the sorrel, heavy cream, and remaining 1 tablespoon butter to the blender. Blend quickly until incorporated, about 2 minutes. Transfer to a large bowl and add salt to taste. Cover and chill for 2 hours before serving.

Wine pairing: This pairs beautifully with the mineral fruitiness of a medium-bodied dry Tokaji wine, like Hárslevelű or Furmint.

In the spring and summer, Hungarians are overrun with an abundance of sour cherries. There are two options: make soup or make liquor. Meggyleves is one of the most iconic Hungarian soups, meant to be served cold in the heat of summer. Because of the unique balance of sweet and tangy, plus the warm hug of cinnamon, this is one of the rare soups that works equally well as a first course or a dessert. For the true Hungarian summer experience, grab the beach chairs, make a circle, and serve this soup with freshly cut peppers and slices of really good bread.

Serves 6 to 8

Meggyleves (Sour Cherry Soup)

Combine the sugar, red wine, vinegar, cinnamon stick, bay leaf, lemon zest, a big pinch of salt, and 5 cups water in a large Dutch oven. Bring to a boil over high heat, then immediately reduce to a low simmer and cook for 5 minutes. Add the pitted cherries. Cover and continue to simmer for 5 more minutes. Remove from the heat and let the soup cool completely. Once cool, slowly whisk in the buttermilk. Chill in the fridge for 2 hours or up to 24 hours. Serve in chilled glasses.

Wine pairing: Pair the Meggyleves with an off-dry (félszáraz) Hárslevelű or Furmint or with a fruit-forward white wine, like Rajnai Rizling or Tramini.

¼ cup sugar

½ cup red wine (whatever you have)

1 teaspoon red wine vinegar

1 cinnamon stick

1 dried bay leaf

Zest of 1 lemon

Kosher salt

1½ pounds sour cherries, pitted

1 cup full-fat buttermilk

Bableves is a Hungarian bean soup that's typically made with pork or smoked ham hocks, kind of a heritage version of beans and franks. This version strays from tradition; instead of simmering the beans with pork, I like to schmear a generous amount of 'nduja over toast for a big, smoky, savory crouton that soaks in the broth and infuses lots of flavor.

Serves 4

Bableves

FOR THE BEANS

2 tablespoons canola oil

1 large carrot, diced

2 celery stalks, diced

1 medium yellow onion, diced

Kosher salt

3 garlic cloves, smashed

½ pound butter beans

4 cups vegetable or chicken stock, store-bought or homemade (page 196)

2 dried bay leaves

TO PLATE

Unsalted butter

1 small loaf crusty bread, sliced 1 inch thick

1 garlic clove

6 ounces 'nduja, room temperature

Extra-virgin olive oil

8 fresh lovage or parsley leaves

Make the beans: Heat the canola oil in a medium heavy-bottomed saucepan over medium-low heat. When the oil shimmers, add the carrot, celery, and onion. Lightly salt the vegetables and cook, stirring occasionally, until they're starting to become translucent, about 6 minutes. Add the garlic and cook, stirring, for 2 minutes. Add the beans, stock, and bay leaves. Bring to a boil, then quickly reduce the heat to low. Cover the saucepan and simmer the beans for 45 minutes to 1 hour. Check on them periodically for tenderness. They should be soft but with a little bite. Season the beans and stock with salt as needed.

To plate: Prepare four shallow bowls. Melt a large knob of butter in a large nonstick skillet over medium heat. Working in batches, fry the sliced bread on both sides until golden brown and bubbling with butter, about 4 minutes total. Lightly rub each slice of bread with the garlic clove. Schmear about 1 tablespoon of the 'nduja across the bread or go easy for a less spicy bite. Place a slice of toast in each bowl. Ladle 1 cup of beans over the toast plus some additional stock. Garnish with a glug of olive oil and the lovage leaves.

Wine pairing: Bableves could pair beautifully with a light red, like Pinot Noir, or with a more medium-bodied and acid-driven red, like Kékfrankos.

This soup is inspired by my best friend, Daniel, who got me hooked on it. Styria is a mountainous state in Austria, bordering Slovenia and near Hungary, and the food traditions lean a little rustic. Without question, it's the best pumpkin soup I've ever had, warm and filling and incredibly simple to make. Every time Red Kuri squash comes into season in the fall, this is the first thing on my to-do list. It's a light ingredient list, but everything supports the squash, letting it fully shine.

Serves 8

Styrian Pumpkin Soup

Heat the butter and canola oil in a large Dutch oven over low heat until the butter is melted. Add the onion plus a pinch of kosher salt. Sauté, stirring occasionally, until the onion is uniformly golden brown and starting to caramelize, 10 to 15 minutes. Be careful not to let it burn. Add the garlic and cook, stirring, for 1 to 2 minutes, until fragrant. Add the stock, squash, paprika, and bay leaf. Bring to a simmer and continue to cook for 30 to 45 minutes, until the squash is very tender. Transfer the soup to a blender, working in batches as needed, and blend on high speed until smooth. Transfer back to the pot off heat and stir in the pumpkin seed oil and heavy cream.

To plate: Divide the soup among bowls. Garnish with flaky salt (crushing between your fingers) and a drizzle of olive oil.

Wine pairing: Pairs nicely with a medium-bodied aromatic white wine with light oak, like Hárslevelű or Rajnai Rizling.

1 tablespoon unsalted butter

2 tablespoons canola oil

1 large yellow onion, thinly sliced

Kosher salt

2 garlic cloves, minced

1 quart vegetable or chicken stock, store-bought or homemade (page 196)

1 pound Red Kuri or Hokkaido squash, peeled, seeded, and cut into 1-inch cubes

½ teaspoon sweet Hungarian paprika

1 dried bay leaf

1 tablespoon pumpkin seed oil

1 cup heavy cream

TO PLATE

Flaky sea salt

Extra-virgin olive oil

Borscht (page 65) and
Styrian Pumpkin Soup (page 63)

This deep green borscht is inspired by one of my favorite food writers, Olia Hercules, who is an expert in eastern European cooking. It's a perfect picture of spring in a bowl, made with so many herbs, loaded with vegetal flavors from chard and beets, and featuring a shoulder of lamb cooked until it's falling apart. This is a perfect rustic soup to serve straight from the pot, either on the table or out in the garden.

Serves 6 to 8

Lorscht (Lamb Borscht)

Make the lamb: Stir together the salt and cumin in a small bowl. Rub the lamb shoulder all over with the salt mixture. This can be done a day ahead and the lamb refrigerated, uncovered.

Heat the canola oil in a large Dutch oven over medium heat. When the oil shimmers, use tongs to carefully lower in the lamb shoulder. Sear it on all sides so a nice golden brown crust develops, about 15 minutes. Transfer the lamb to a rimmed baking sheet to rest. Reduce the heat to medium-low and add the fennel and onion. Cook, stirring often, until translucent and fragrant, about 4 minutes. Add the garlic and cook, stirring, for 1 minute. Add the beets, chard, and cabbage and stir until the greens start to wilt. Return the lamb (and its juices that have collected on the baking sheet) to the Dutch oven and cover with the chicken stock. Bring to a gentle simmer. Cover and cook for 1 to 2 hours, until the lamb is falling apart and super tender. Use a wooden spoon or tongs to break the meat into large chunks. Taste the broth for seasoning and add salt as needed.

Make the green sauce: Stir together all the sauce ingredients in a medium bowl. Add the sauce to the soup, gently swirling it around so it sits on the surface. Ladle into individual bowls and serve.

Wine pairing: Try the lorscht with a full-bodied volcanic white, like an oak-aged Furmint or Juhfark, or with an aromatic skin-contact (orange) Tramini or similar.

* Remove the lamb from the fridge 1 hour before cooking, to come to room temperature.

FOR THE LAMB

3 tablespoons kosher salt, plus more as needed

1 tablespoon ground cumin

1 (3- to 4-pound) boneless lamb shoulder*

3 tablespoons canola oil

1 large fennel bulb, fronds reserved, finely diced

1 medium yellow onion, finely diced

2 garlic cloves, minced

1½ pounds yellow beets, peeled and finely diced

2 bunches of Swiss chard, chopped

1 small head of green cabbage, halved and thinly sliced

3 quarts chicken stock, store-bought or homemade (page 196)

FOR THE GREEN SAUCE

2 cups chopped fresh dill

1 cup chopped fresh parsley

1 cup chopped fresh mint

½ cup chopped fresh cilantro

1 garlic clove, minced

1 cup extra-virgin olive oil

1 tablespoon fresh lemon juice

1 teaspoon kosher salt

This is a dumpling recipe disguised as a soup. These dumplings can easily hop pots, starring in chicken soup, nestling alongside brothy clams, or just simmering until puffy and served alongside Short Rib Gulyás (page 94). I came up with this particular soup because I wanted a way to highlight the dumplings themselves in a fresh spring-forward, delicate stock. The radishes and their greens have a mild peppery flavor that soaks into the dumplings as they simmer for a perfect bowl.

Serves 4

Radish Soup & Semolina Dumplings

FOR THE DUMPLINGS

1 cup semolina flour

2 tablespoons unsalted butter

1 large egg

2 teaspoons kosher salt

1 quart vegetable or chicken stock, store-bought or homemade (page 196)

FOR THE SOUP

1 tablespoon canola oil

5 celery stalks, finely diced

1 medium yellow onion, finely diced

Kosher salt

12 breakfast radishes, leaves and radish separated

TO PLATE

Flaky sea salt and freshly ground pepper

Extra-virgin olive oil

Make the dumplings: Bring 2 cups water to a boil in a small saucepan over medium heat. Slowly whisk in the semolina flour. It should become thick very quickly. Continue to cook for 2 minutes and use a wooden spoon to stir constantly. Remove from the heat and whisk in the butter, egg, and salt until fully incorporated. Once the semolina mixture is cool enough to handle, use a 3-tablespoon cookie scoop to scoop dumplings. Don't worry about rolling them smooth; the jagged texture is ideal. Set on a rimmed baking sheet and continue scooping until you've used up all the dough, about 16 dumplings.

Meanwhile, bring the stock to a simmer in a medium saucepan over medium-low heat. Working in two batches, carefully lower the dumplings into the stock and let simmer for about 6 minutes, until they float to the surface. Use a wide slotted spoon or spider strainer to divide the dumplings among shallow bowls. Save the stock for the next step.

Make the soup: Heat the canola oil in a medium skillet over medium heat. When the oil shimmers, add the celery, onion, and a big pinch of kosher salt. Cook, stirring occasionally, until the veggies are translucent but not taking on any color, about 5 minutes. Scrape the veggies into the stock and bring to a boil over medium heat. Meanwhile, use a mandoline or sharp knife to thinly slice the radishes into small rounds. Add the radish greens to the soup and stir until they just start to wilt. Stir the radish rounds into the soup.

To plate: Remove the pot from the heat and ladle the soup over the dumplings. Garnish with flaky salt and plenty of pepper, followed by a drizzle of olive oil.

Wine pairing: Try the soup with an unoaked and fresh white wine (Olaszrizling, Zöldveltelini, Egri Csillag, or similar).

This is a soup that doesn't exist from a town that doesn't exist. What I mean is it's so specifically tied to one region that if you went to Hungary and asked for it, almost no one would know what you're talking about. And the one and only time I had it was in a very tiny town named Polonya, which is so hidden on the map that if you went to Hungary and asked for it, almost no one would know what you're talking about.

Michael and I went to meet my friend Zsuzsa, a Hungarian food writer, who is wildly eccentric and a lot of fun. It was a six-hour drive through the country to get to Polonya, and Zsuzsa specifically warned us to avoid the sunflower field along the way. But they're my favorite flowers and I couldn't resist their siren call. So it was no surprise when our car broke down in the middle of the field because our tire went into a big ditch. After a dreamy photo shoot in the flowers (I try my best to appreciate beauty even in crisis), we pushed the car over to a house in the distance. There we met a family of Ukrainian cigarette smugglers who didn't speak any English, but through careful miming we agreed that they would change the tire. And since we didn't have any cash on us, we bartered the dobos torte (a Hungarian cake) we had in the backseat.

We finally made it to the town and settled in at Zsuzsa's bed-and-breakfast, where she made this soup for dinner. The broth is pared down and simple, just veggies and stock, which means the pasta is the star of the show. Thin strips of homemade pasta dough get twisted and then tied into a loose knot. It's such a special shape and texture that I've never experienced anywhere else. Making pasta by hand is a process to settle into, with a good album, maybe some helping hands, and a bottle of wine to make it go faster. But the journey—just like our odyssey to Polonya—is totally worth it.

Serves 6 to 8

Knot Soup

Make the pasta: Process the semolina, egg yolks, whole egg, olive oil, and salt in a food processor until just combined, about 1 minute. With the processor running, slowly stream in the cold water until a ball of dough forms. You might not have to use all the water. If you overwater the dough, just add a little more semolina until it comes back together.

Lightly flour a work surface, turn out the dough, and knead for 5 minutes, until smooth. Flatten the dough into a disk and wrap tightly in plastic. Let sit at room temperature for 1 hour to rest.

Line a rimmed baking sheet with parchment paper and dust it lightly with flour.

You can either roll out the pasta with a rolling pin or a pasta machine. Cut the dough into quarters. Starting with one quarter, flatten the dough with your hands. Roll out the pasta to ⅛ inch or as thin as you

FOR THE PASTA

1⅔ cups semolina flour, plus extra for the work surface

2 large egg yolks

1 large egg

1 tablespoon extra-virgin olive oil

1 teaspoon kosher salt

½ cup ice-cold water

FOR THE SOUP

1 tablespoon canola oil

1 tablespoon unsalted butter

RECIPE CONTINUES

2 medium yellow onions, finely diced

4 medium carrots, finely diced

4 celery stalks, finely diced

Kosher salt

8 cups vegetable or chicken stock, store-bought or homemade (page 196)

TO PLATE

Extra-virgin olive oil

Flaky sea salt

can get it. On a pasta machine you will want to work your way down through the numbers (refer to your manual). Once you've rolled out the dough, cut the sheet into 5 × 1-inch strips. Hold 1 strip by the ends and twist 5 or 6 times for a twirl. Pinch each end to seal and then tie a loose knot with the twisted strip. Lay the knotted pasta on the prepared baking sheet. Repeat this process with the remaining dough. You don't have to use all of the knotted pasta for this recipe. You can freeze any extra on a clean baking sheet and then pack into plastic zip-top bags to freeze for up to 2 weeks.

Prepare the soup: Heat the canola oil and butter in a large Dutch oven over low heat. Once the butter is melted, add the onions, carrots, and celery and season with salt. Cook the vegetables, stirring often, until tender and translucent but not taking on any color, about 10 minutes. Add the stock and increase the heat to medium. Bring to a simmer, then add the pasta and cook for 2 minutes. Remove from the heat, taste, and adjust the seasoning if needed.

To plate: Portion the soup into individual serving bowls and garnish with a drizzle of olive oil and a sprinkle of flaky salt.

Wine pairing: This pairs nicely with a medium-bodied dry Tokaji wine, like Hárslevelű or Furmint.

Nokedli is the Hungarian answer to spaetzle, plump eggy nubs that are somewhere between a noodle and a dumpling. Grandma Agi used to serve this in plain chicken broth or alongside paprikash as a starch. This version, which is very popular at the restaurant, is like a turbo-charged chicken noodle soup. We serve it starting in the fall, and every week we go through bushels of dill, pounds of nokedli, and gallons of chicken stock. The nokedli are dense and chewy, the perfect bite in every spoonful. But dill is the real star here, so use a heavy hand. It's a short ingredient list, so get the best of everything (homemade chicken stock, page 196, makes all the difference) for the best bowl of soup.

Serves 4

Nokedli in Chicken Broth with So Much Dill

Whisk together the flour and salt in a large bowl. In a medium bowl, whisk together the eggs and milk. Pour the wet ingredients into the dry ingredients and whisk until fully incorporated. The mixture should resemble a thick pancake batter. Let rest for 30 minutes to thicken.

Meanwhile, bring a large pot of heavily salted water to a rolling boil over high heat. Once your water is boiling, set a colander over it. Make sure you have an exit strategy ready: a large bowl and a slotted spoon will do.

Working in batches, push the batter through the colander using a bench scraper or metal spatula. The batter should drip through the colander and into the water. Let cook for 30 seconds, until the nokedli pop to the surface. Use a wide slotted spoon or spider strainer to transfer nokedli to a clean large bowl. Repeat with the remaining batter.

Pour the chicken stock into a large Dutch oven over high heat and add nokedli. Bring to a rolling boil, then immediately turn off the heat. Taste for seasoning and adjust as needed. Ladle the soup into individual bowls or mugs and garnish with so much dill and a little bit of olive oil.

Wine pairing: Pair the nokedli with a fuller-bodied Somlói white wine aged in oak or with a similar savory-salty fuller white.

2 cups all-purpose flour

½ teaspoon kosher salt, plus more as needed

4 large eggs

⅔ cup whole milk

8 cups chicken stock, store-bought or homemade (page 196)

1 cup roughly chopped fresh dill

Extra-virgin olive oil

Hungarian cuisine is meant to stick to your ribs, so the portions are big and the dishes are hearty. This chapter also explores flavors and ingredients (including vegetarian meals) that have a lighter touch without compromising on flavor.

Mains

All the women on my dad's side of the family have a version of stuffed cabbage, all differentiated by a single ingredient or a small measurement. Grandma Agi had a version, her sister-in-law (also Agi) had a version, my dad's aunt Simi had a version. They all felt like theirs was the best and the right way. In my version, I pack the cabbage with lots of fresh produce for something that would feel equally satisfying and filling in the middle of winter or the height of summer.

Serves 6

Stuffed Cabbage

½ pound slab bacon,*
store-bought or homemade
(page 200), chopped

2 medium yellow onions,
chopped

4 celery stalks, chopped

2 medium fennel bulbs,
chopped

2 large heads of green cabbage,
1 head thinly sliced and 1 head
separated into leaves

2 garlic cloves, chopped

Kosher salt

4 cups vegetable or chicken
stock, store-bought or
homemade (page 196)

TO PLATE

Flaky sea salt and freshly
ground black pepper (optional)

Sour cream (optional)

Extra-virgin olive oil (optional)

Chopped fresh dill (optional)

Pickled shallots (optional)

*Leave out the bacon to make this vegetarian

Preheat the oven to 350°F. Line a plate with paper towels.

To make the filling, place the bacon in a large Dutch oven over medium heat and cook for 10 minutes, stirring occasionally, until the bacon has rendered out most of its fat and is golden brown. Remove the bacon using a slotted spoon and transfer to the paper towels to drain. Add the onions, celery, fennel, and sliced cabbage to the Dutch oven. Cook the vegetables in the bacon fat, stirring occasionally, until tender and translucent, about 5 minutes. Add the garlic and toast, stirring, for 1 minute. Stir in the drained bacon and season the mixture with a pinch of salt. Remove from the heat and let cool slightly. Transfer the mixture to a food processor and pulse about 4 times until it's finely chopped.

Prepare an ice-water bath in a large bowl. Bring a large pot of water to a boil over high heat. Submerge the cabbage leaves in the water until translucent and vibrant, about 5 minutes. Use tongs to plunge the leaves into the ice-water bath. Let chill for 2 minutes to stop the cooking.

Remove the cabbage leaves from the water and squeeze the excess water out of them. Working one at a time, lay a leaf on a cutting board and slice diagonally on either side of the stem to remove it. Place a heaping tablespoon of filling in the center of the leaf. Fold the sides in and roll the cabbage like a burrito. Line up the stuffed cabbages in a 9 × 13-inch baking dish. Once the dish is filled, pour in the stock. Cover the dish tightly with aluminum foil. Bake for 20 to 30 minutes, until the cabbage and stock are steaming hot. Remove from the oven and uncover.

To plate: Spoon 2 cabbage rolls with some stock into a shallow bowl. Sprinkle with flaky salt and pepper. Dollop a small amount of sour cream on top and drizzle with olive oil. Finish with fresh dill and pickled shallots. All these toppings are optional and can be added in any order.

Wine pairing: The stuffed cabbage pairs beautifully with a medium-bodied fiery red wine from the volcanic soils of Eger.

This schnitzel mimics my Rántott Hús (page 89) but is fully vegetarian. It also happens to be a good disguise to trick the veggie-averse into getting their daily dose. I like turnips here because they're sturdy and substantial enough to hold up to frying but still tender enough to slice into (plus, I just really love turnips). This is a great pairing with many of the sides in this book for a vegetarian feast.

Serves 4

Turnip Schnitzel

Set a wire rack in a rimmed baking sheet. Lay your sliced turnips on the rack and lightly season with a few pinches of salt. Set aside.

Combine the bread crumbs, parsley, and 1 teaspoon salt in a food processor. Pulse 6 to 8 times, until the crumbs are fine and have turned a pale green. Transfer to a medium shallow bowl. Create a breading station: Place the rack of salted turnips on your work surface. Next to the turnips, place a medium bowl of flour, a medium bowl of beaten eggs, and the bowl of bread crumbs.

Designate one hand to be your dry hand and use it to dip one turnip slice in the flour. Make sure it's fully coated. Shake any excess flour off. Use your designated wet hand to dredge the floured turnip in the egg. Remove from the egg, letting excess drip off, and transfer it to the bread crumbs. Finally, use your dry hand to toss the turnip in the bread crumbs. Do not pack on the crumbs. Transfer the turnip back to the wire rack and repeat with the remaining turnips.

Line a large plate with paper towels. Heat the canola oil in a large sauté pan or cast-iron skillet over medium heat. When the oil shimmers, carefully place 2 or 3 turnips in the pan. Fry the turnips until golden brown, about 2 minutes per side. Remove with tongs and set on the paper towels to drain. Repeat with the remaining turnips.

To garnish, place the lemon halves cut side down in a small nonstick skillet over medium-high heat. Caramelize the lemons for about 5 minutes, until the lemon is slightly charred and glossy. Serve 2 turnips on each plate and sprinkle with flaky salt. Nestle a charred lemon half next to each pair of turnips.

Wine pairing: This pairs nicely with a fuller-bodied Cabernet Franc, Merlot, or Syrah from the south of Hungary.

2 large turnips, peeled and sliced ¼ inch thick for 8 slices total

Kosher salt

2 cups plain bread crumbs

2 packed cups fresh parsley leaves

1 cup all-purpose flour

2 large eggs, beaten

1 cup canola oil

TO GARNISH

2 lemons, halved

Flaky sea salt

I think of nokedli as the sidekick in every story. It's always riding sidecar to the main dish. But it's so delicious that I feel it deserves its own moment. This spin on a cacio e pepe has all the joy of the cheesy buttered noodles you ate as a kid but with slightly grown-up flavors. I like to serve it on a really big platter and absolutely shower it with a mountain of cheese, the coronation nokedli deserves.

Serves 4

Nokedli Cacio e Pepe

FOR THE NOKEDLI

2 cups all-purpose flour

½ teaspoon kosher salt, plus more as needed

4 large eggs

⅔ cup whole milk

FOR THE SAUCE

1 stick (8 tablespoons) unsalted butter

½ tablespoon freshly ground black pepper, plus more to garnish

1 teaspoon kosher salt

1 ounce Grana Padano, plus more as needed

Extra-virgin olive oil

Make the nokedli: Whisk together the flour and ½ teaspoon of salt in a large bowl. In a medium bowl, whisk together the eggs and milk. Pour the wet ingredients into the dry ingredients and whisk until fully incorporated. The mixture should resemble a thick pancake batter. Let rest for 30 minutes to thicken.

Meanwhile, bring a large pot of heavily salted water to a rolling boil over high heat. Once your water is boiling, set a colander over it. Make sure you have an exit strategy ready: a large bowl and a slotted spoon will do.

Working in batches, push the batter through the colander using a bench scraper or metal spatula. The batter should drip through the colander and into the water. Let cook for 30 seconds, until the nokedli pop to the surface. Use a wide slotted spoon or spider strainer to transfer the nokedli to a clean large bowl. Repeat with the remaining batter. Reserve 1½ cups of the starchy cooking water.

Make the sauce: Pour 1 cup of the reserved cooking water into a large sauté pan and set over medium heat. Add the butter, pepper, and salt and bring to a simmer. Reduce the liquid by half, until the sauce just begins to thicken, 2 to 3 minutes. Remove from the heat and add the nokedli. Stir to fully coat the dumplings in the sauce. It should be creamy and slightly glossy. Add a splash or two of the remaining cooking water as needed to loosen.

Immediately transfer the nokedli to a serving platter. Shake the platter to even out the dumplings. Grate the Grana Padano all over the plate (it should be grand and messy!). Cover it with extra pepper and a drizzle of olive oil before serving.

Wine pairing: This pairs beautifully with a bright, medium-bodied, acid-driven dry red like Kékfrankos, Egri Bikavér, or Syrah.

I couldn't possibly write a Hungarian cookbook and not include the most famous Hungarian dish. Needless to say, Agi served this a lot when I was growing up, usually with a bowl of sour cream and a mountain of egg noodles. I remember playing in her den and hearing the sizzle of chicken and onions hitting hot oil. The scent of paprika lingered in her house and it always smelled like comfort to me. This version is pretty faithful to Agi's recipe. I like to serve it with a good, soft bread and plenty of slices of fresh bell or sweet peppers. And when I have leftovers, I like to shred the chicken and roll it in a warm palacsinta (see page 177) with a spoonful of sauce.

Serves 4

Good Ol'-Fashioned Chicken Paprikash

3 to 4 pounds bone-in, skin-on chicken thighs

Kosher salt

¼ cup canola oil

2 medium yellow onions, halved and thinly sliced

1 tablespoon tomato paste

1 tablespoon smoked paprika

1 tablespoon hot paprika

2 cups chicken stock, store-bought or homemade (page 196)

½ cup sour cream

Spread out the thighs on a large plate or tray and pat dry with paper towels. Season on both sides with 1 tablespoon salt.

Heat the canola oil in a large skillet over medium heat. When the oil shimmers, add the chicken and cook for 4 minutes on each side until golden brown. You're not looking to fully cook the chicken here, just getting some color on it. Transfer the chicken back to the plate.

Add the onions to the skillet and cook for 10 to 15 minutes, stirring frequently, until soft and starting to caramelize. Add the tomato paste and stir until the onions are fully coated and the paste begins to stick to the skillet, about 2 minutes. Stir in both paprikas and toast for 5 seconds, until very fragrant. Immediately pour in the stock and stir to scrape up any browned bits on the bottom of the pot. Nestle the chicken back in the skillet. Bring the liquid to a boil, then reduce to a low simmer. Cook for 30 to 45 minutes, until the chicken is tender and cooked through. Remove from the heat. Taste for seasoning and adjust if needed.

Vigorously whisk the sour cream in a small bowl until it's light and airy. Dollop over the chicken or serve on the side. Serve the chicken paprikash directly from the skillet.

Wine pairing: Try the classic pairing of paprikash with Egri Bikavér or with another medium-bodied fiery red wine from northern Hungary.

While I have a faithful version of Chicken Paprikash on page 82, this is my very unfaithful version. There's nothing wrong with chicken paprikash—it's perfect. But there's also nothing I love more than a good roast chicken. I would die for roast chicken. This one is brined in buttermilk, which keeps it really juicy and tender. The milk fat on the skin also gives perfect, even browning, which feels like a cheat, but we'll take the win. Once it comes out, the chicken gets drenched in an acidic paprika dressing to mingle with all the fattiness. Pops of fresh dill add a welcome herbiness and bursts of color. This is a total showstopper, but if you're like me, you'll want to just stand in your underwear and eat it over a trash can.

Serves 4

Unfaithful Roast Chicken

1 (3- to 4-pound) chicken, spatchcocked (see "On Spatchcocking," page 86)

Kosher salt

2 cups full-fat buttermilk

FOR THE DRESSING

2 garlic cloves, minced

2 cups extra-virgin olive oil

Juice of 4 lemons

2 tablespoons smoked paprika

1 tablespoon hot paprika

TO PLATE

1 cup chopped fresh dill

Flaky sea salt

Freshly ground black pepper

Do a day ahead: Place the chicken in a large bowl or airtight container. Liberally season all over with kosher salt. Pour the buttermilk over the chicken and massage into all the nooks and crannies. Cover tightly with plastic wrap or seal the container with a lid and refrigerate for 24 hours.

Pull the chicken from the fridge an hour or so before you plan to roast it. Preheat the oven to 425°F.

Use tongs to lift the chicken and let the excess buttermilk drip off, then transfer to a large cast-iron skillet or a rimmed baking sheet. Dab the chicken lightly with paper towels to remove any pools of buttermilk. Place the chicken in the oven and roast for 20 minutes, until golden brown. Reduce the oven temperature to 400°F and continue roasting for about 10 minutes, until the chicken reaches an internal temperature of 160°F in the thickest part of the breast. Remove from the oven and let rest for 10 minutes in the skillet.

Meanwhile, make the dressing: Whisk together all the ingredients in a large bowl until thoroughly combined.

To plate: Transfer the chicken to a cutting board and cut into 6 pieces (2 breasts, 2 thighs, 2 drumsticks), then return to the skillet. Spoon the dressing over the chicken. Garnish with the dill, a sprinkle of flaky salt, and plenty of pepper before serving directly from the skillet.

Wine pairing: Try pairing the roast chicken with a sparkling white wine, an oak-aged dry Tokaji, or a skin-contact (orange) wine from Olaszrizling.

ON SPATCHCOCKING

You can ask your butcher to spatchcock a chicken for you; that's the easy way out. But if you want to do it yourself, it's just two simple steps. Find the backbone (on the opposite side of the breast meat) and use sharp kitchen shears to cut along either side of the bone to remove it. Flip the chicken breast side up and use two hands to press on the center of the breasts until the bone cracks and the chicken lays flat.

ON PEELING TOMATOES

Cut a small X on the bottom of the tomato, slicing through the skin but leaving the flesh intact. Prepare an ice-water bath. Bring a saucepan of water to boil over high heat, then carefully lower in the tomato. Simmer for 1 minute, then immediately remove the tomato with a slotted spoon and plunge it into the ice-water bath. Once it's cool enough to handle, use your fingers to peel the skin off.

A lot of Hungarian proteins are either fried or stewed—very heavy-duty cooking. But I wanted to explore what a lighter touch might look like. Pork with peppers and onions is such a classic combo, so pairing these pork chops with lecsó, here in the form of a roasted pepper sauce, felt natural. Some charred spring onions balance everything out, but use leeks or scallions in the colder months when spring onions aren't in season. Ideally, though, this is a perfect recipe to be enjoyed outside in great weather.

Serves 4

Pork Chop with Lecsó & Onions

Make the pork: Generously season the pork chops with kosher salt 1 day before cooking. Set a wire rack in a rimmed baking sheet, arrange the pork chops on the rack, and refrigerate, uncovered, for 24 hours or up to 48 hours.

Make the lecsó sauce: Combine the peppers, tomato, vinegar, and paprika in a blender. With the blender running on high speed, slowly drizzle in the olive oil. Season with kosher salt to taste. Set aside.

Heat the canola oil in a large cast-iron skillet over medium heat. When the oil shimmers, set the pork chops in the pan on their side to render the fat cap. They should stand on their own, but you can also lean them on the sides of the skillet. Sear until the fat cap is crispy and golden brown, 10 to 15 minutes. Turn the pork chops to lay flat. Increase the heat to high and cook for 3 to 4 minutes on each side, until golden brown and the pork registers 135°F on an instant-read thermometer. Transfer the pork to a platter, lightly tented with foil, to rest for 10 minutes. Let the pan cool slightly and wipe it out with a rag.

Return the skillet to high heat. Add the spring onions, working in batches, and sear until they just begin to char, about 2 minutes on each side. Season with kosher salt and remove from the pan.

To plate: Divide the pork among plates. Season with flaky salt and pepper, then drizzle with olive oil. Spoon some lecsó sauce over the pork and garnish with the spring onions.

Wine pairing: Pair the pork chops with an oak-aged Tokaji Furmint or with another deep, mineral-driven white wine.

FOR THE PORK
4 (12- to 14-ounce) pork chops or T-bones

Kosher salt

1 tablespoon canola oil

FOR THE LECSÓ SAUCE
3 red bell peppers, roasted and peeled (see page 33)

1 small tomato, peeled (see "On Peeling Tomatoes," opposite)

2 teaspoons sherry vinegar

1 teaspoon smoked paprika

½ cup extra-virgin olive oil

Kosher salt

FOR THE ONIONS
8 to 10 spring onions

Kosher salt

TO PLATE
Flaky sea salt

Freshly ground black pepper

Extra-virgin olive oil

Even though chicken paprikash is the signature Hungarian dish, this is what Grandma Agi made constantly. Rántott hús frying on the stove is the smell I most associate with walking into her house, and I have a lot of memories of cutlets draining on oil-soaked paper towels. She served hers with slices of lemon, alongside nokedli and her cauliflower mush. It's the one dish I most associate with my childhood. Here, the cutlet with seasoned bread crumbs stays faithful to Agi but is helped along with a pickled pepper sauce and sweet candied lemons. It's a rare dish that's both comforting enough for family dinner and impressive enough for a party.

Serves 4

Rántott Hús (Fried Pork Cutlet)

Make the candied lemon: Slice the lemon as thin as you can with a serrated knife and place in a small heatproof container. Combine the sugar with 1 cup water in a small saucepan. Bring to a boil over high heat and cook until all the sugar is dissolved. Immediately pour over the lemon. Let the mixture cool completely, then cover and let sit at room temperature for as long as possible. This can be done up to 1 day in advance. Just before serving, remove the lemon slices from the syrup* and transfer to a plate.

Make the bread crumbs: Whisk together the bread crumbs, parsley, oregano, garlic powder, and kosher salt in a large shallow bowl. Set aside.

Make the pork: Begin by pounding out the pork loins. (You can ask your butcher to do this for you.) Don't go crazy, just a few good whacks with a mallet to thin them out a bit. Season the loins generously with kosher salt and let sit for up to 1 hour.

To bread the pork loins, give yourself ample space. Clear the counter! Whisk the eggs in a large shallow bowl. In a separate but similar bowl, shake the flour into an even layer. Place the bread crumb bowl next to the eggs. Set a wire rack in a rimmed baking sheet and place it next to the bread crumbs. This is your order of operations.

*Save that syrup for cocktails, lemonade, or boosting your seltzer. Store in an airtight container in the refrigerator for up to 1 month.

FOR THE CANDIED LEMON

1 lemon

1 cup sugar

FOR THE BREAD CRUMBS

2 cups plain bread crumbs

½ tablespoon dried parsley

½ tablespoon dried oregano

1 teaspoon garlic powder

1 teaspoon kosher salt

FOR THE PORK

4 (6-ounce) boneless center-cut pork loins

Kosher salt

3 large eggs

1 cup all-purpose flour

2 cups canola oil

FOR THE SAUCE

2 tablespoons canola oil

2 garlic cloves, thinly sliced

½ cup dry white wine

RECIPE CONTINUES

1 cup chicken stock, store-bought or homemade (page 196)

8 whole pickled peppers, such as guindillas

2 tablespoons unsalted butter, chilled and cubed

Freshly ground black pepper

TO GARNISH
Extra-virgin olive oil

Flaky sea salt

Designate one "dry" hand and use it to dredge the first loin in the flour, then shake off the excess. Using your designated "wet" hand, dunk the loin in the egg and let the excess drip off. Repeat in the flour and egg dredge one more time, sticking to the dry and wet hand method. Finally, dunk the loin in the bread crumbs with your dry hand. Do not pack the bread crumbs on! Just give the loin a light toss so it's fully coated. Transfer to the wire rack, then continue dredging the remaining loins. Let the coated loins rest on the rack for about 30 minutes.

Meanwhile, make the sauce: Heat the 2 tablespoons of canola oil in a medium saucepan over medium-low heat. When the oil shimmers, add the sliced garlic and toast until it just starts to turn golden, about 2 minutes. Remove from the heat and add the white wine. Place the saucepan over medium heat and simmer until reduced by half, about 5 minutes. Add the stock, pickled peppers, butter, and plenty of black pepper. Simmer, swirling the saucepan occasionally, until the sauce thickens just slightly, about 3 minutes. Remove from the heat and cover to keep warm.

To fry the loins, heat the 2 cups canola oil in a large skillet over medium heat. Let the oil get to temperature, then sprinkle in a few bread crumbs to test. If they sink immediately, the oil isn't hot enough. If they burn immediately, the oil is too hot. If they gently bubble and float, it's time to fry. Working in batches, carefully lower the breaded cutlets into the oil. Fry for about 2 minutes on each side, until golden brown. Transfer to a clean wire rack to let the excess oil drip off. Continue frying the remaining loins.

Arrange the pork loins on a serving platter. Spoon the sauce over the pork and garnish with candied lemon slices, olive oil, and flaky salt.

Wine pairing: Pair the rántott hús with a fuller, savory white wine from Somló (like Furmint) or with a dry medium-bodied Cabernet Franc or similar.

Brisket is *the* Jewish holiday staple. In our family, Nana Arlene was in charge of making it. Like Taylor Swift, Arlene's brisket had eras. There was a raisin phase, a mushroom phase, sometimes ketchup, always onions, and the one constant was Lipton onion soup mix. For this version I wanted to replicate that nostalgic smell and flavor but keep it really simple with just a few ingredients. Brisket is always better the next day, so I like to make it a day or two in advance and reheat when it's time. And personally, I like to pull it apart rather than slice, but you can be like Arlene and whip out the electric knife. No question, though, the best part is the leftovers, which make really good sandwiches on toasted challah (page 52).

Serves 8 to 10

Brisket

1 (6-pound) beef brisket, with most of the fat trimmed

¼ cup plus ½ tablespoon kosher salt

6 medium yellow onions, quartered

3 tablespoons canola oil

1 tablespoon ground cumin

2 tablespoons smoked paprika

2 cups golden raisins

2 cups ketchup

¼ cup sherry vinegar

Preheat the oven to 400°F.

Rub the brisket with ¼ cup of the salt, covering it evenly. Set a wire rack in a rimmed baking sheet and place the brisket on top. Transfer to the refrigerator, uncovered, to rest overnight or for up to 24 hours.

Toss the onions with canola oil, cumin, and the remaining ½ tablespoon salt in a large bowl. Spread the onions evenly on a rimmed baking sheet. Roast for about 1 hour, until they're just starting to char. They should look slightly blackened and deflated. Let them cool completely, then transfer to a 9 × 13-inch baking dish. Cover tightly with plastic wrap and store in the fridge overnight.

The next day, preheat the oven to 300°F.

Pull the brisket and onions from the fridge. Rub the brisket all over with the paprika. Set the brisket in the baking dish over the onions, fat side up (whatever fat is remaining). Whisk together the raisins, ketchup, and vinegar in a medium bowl. Pour the raisin mixture over the brisket and cover tightly with aluminum foil.

Transfer to the oven and braise the brisket for 4 to 6 hours. It should be fork-tender, meaning it falls apart with a gentle pull of the fork, and a test bite melts in your mouth. Let sit to cool slightly. You can slice and serve the brisket from here. Or, even better, cool completely, cover tightly with foil, refrigerate, and reheat it the next day.

Wine pairing: Try the brisket with a skin-contact (orange) white wine or with a lighter acid-driven red, like a Kékfrankos from northern Hungary.

Forget everything you know about the American ideal of goulash—this is the real origin of the dish. It's a very slowly braised, hearty, beefy stew that's traditionally served with fresh peppers and bread, although nokedli (see page 80) would also be a perfect starchy side. (Don't tell anyone I said this, but I love egg noodles here too.) In Hungary, they use stewing meat, so the short ribs are my extra touch of decadence for a melt-in-your-mouth experience.

Serves 4

Short Rib Gulyás

1 tablespoon canola oil

Kosher salt

2¼ pounds boneless short ribs, cut in 2-inch pieces

2 large yellow onions, halved

2 tablespoons tomato paste

5 tablespoons sweet Hungarian paprika

2 teaspoons hot paprika or a pinch of cayenne pepper

2 cups dry red wine

1 (28-ounce) can whole peeled tomatoes

½ tablespoon red wine vinegar

2 dried bay leaves

4 cups good beef stock

Heat the canola oil in a large Dutch oven over medium-high heat. Generously salt the ribs on all sides. Working in batches, sear the ribs, turning occasionally, until browned on all sides, 6 to 8 minutes total. The pot shouldn't be crowded or the meat won't brown evenly. Transfer the ribs to a large plate once seared.

In the same pot, arrange the halved onions cut side down. Sear for 6 to 8 minutes, until the onions are charred. (Don't be alarmed if they seem slightly burnt; that's what we want!) Stir in the tomato paste and both paprikas. Wait about 10 seconds to let the spices toast, but not too long or they'll get bitter, then immediately add the wine. Use a wooden spoon to deglaze and scrape up all the flavorful bits from the bottom of the pot. Cook until most of the wine has reduced, about 6 minutes, then add the tomatoes and vinegar. Use the spoon to mash the tomatoes. Add a couple big pinches of salt, the bay leaves, and the stock. Stir to combine.

Nestle the ribs into the liquid. Cover and bring to a simmer over low heat. The beef has to cook low and slow to get perfectly tender, which will take 3 to 4 hours. Once the meat is falling apart and the sauce is dark and thick, taste for seasoning and adjust as needed. I like to serve the short ribs directly from the pot at the table.

Wine pairing: This pairs beautifully with a fuller-bodied dry red like a Cabernet Franc from Villány.

I think the first time I was ever conscious of beef tongue was at Bagel Works, in a strip mall in Boca Raton. It had lime-green walls and a case full of smoked trout and beef tongue. Papa Howie would sometimes order a tongue sandwich with slaw and I couldn't get far enough away from it. It wasn't until my late teens that I discovered tongue for myself, so I understand the aversion. I think it's easy to be afraid of because it's . . . well, a massive tongue. But the flavor and texture remind me a lot of brisket. When cooked properly, it's meltingly tender, and when seasoned well, it's so beautifully flavored. I love it in sandwiches, sliced and seared over a salad, or even just served as a main with some great sides.

Serves 6 to 8

Coriander-Crusted Beef Tongue

Lay a piece of parchment on your work surface. Trace the lid of a large Dutch oven on the parchment and cut out the circle.

Heat ¼ cup of the canola oil in the Dutch oven over medium heat. When the oil shimmers, add the celery, carrots, and onions. Cook the veggies, stirring occasionally, until nicely softened, about 10 minutes. You're not looking to achieve any color on these vegetables! Add a splash of water if they begin to stick.

Add the salt, parsley, peppercorns, bay leaves, and vinegar. Nestle the tongue in the center of the Dutch oven and cover with enough water to just barely submerge the meat. Cover and bring to a boil. Once at a boil, uncover, reduce to a low simmer, and lay the parchment round on top. Continue to cook the tongue for 3 to 4 hours, until fork-tender. Top off with water as needed to keep the tongue submerged.

Use tongs to transfer the tongue to a rimmed baking sheet. Discard the braising liquid. When the tongue is cool enough to handle, peel the outer layer of skin and discard.

Make the rub: Pulse the coriander and black pepper 2 or 3 times in a spice grinder for a very coarse grind. (They can also be ground with a mortar and pestle or crushed with a rolling pin.) Mix together the spices and salt in a small bowl until thoroughly combined. Discard any liquid from the baking sheet and pat the tongue dry with paper towels.

½ cup canola oil

3 celery stalks, roughly chopped

2 medium carrots, roughly chopped

2 medium yellow onions, quartered

1 tablespoon kosher salt

12 fresh parsley sprigs

½ tablespoon black peppercorns

2 dried bay leaves

¼ cup red wine vinegar

1 (4- to 5-pound) beef tongue

FOR THE RUB

6 tablespoons coriander seeds, toasted (see page 209)

3 tablespoons black peppercorns

1 tablespoon kosher salt

RECIPE CONTINUES

Generously sprinkle the spice rub all over and pack onto the tongue.

Heat the remaining ¼ cup of canola oil in a large skillet over medium-high heat. When the oil shimmers, use tongs to lay the tongue in the pan. Sear on all sides until crispy and golden brown, about 20 minutes total. Remove from the skillet and slice before serving.

Wine pairing: Pair this with a lighter, spicier red like Kadarka.

This would probably be a very big no-no in Hungary, maybe even semi-illegal. But I think the paprikash formula—traditionally for chicken only—is so easily adaptable because it's essentially a formula of onions, paprika, and protein. I wanted to create a sauce that would mimic the flavor profile while sticking to the shrimp for a messy finger-licking food. This shell butter enhances the shrimpy flavor beautifully and makes this feel like a true event of a dish.

Shrimp Paprikash

Serves 4 to 6

Make the shell butter: Place the onion halves cut side down in a cast-iron skillet set over high heat. We don't want to use any fat; this is a dry process. Cook until the cut sides are slightly blackened, about 6 minutes, then transfer to a medium saucepan over low heat. Add the butter, shells, garlic, thyme, and salt. Let the butter melt and mingle with the shells and aromatics, swirling the saucepan occasionally, for about 10 minutes. Don't let the butter brown! Set a fine-mesh strainer over a medium bowl and strain the butter, pressing on the shells with the back of a spoon to get any additional flavor out. Cover the shell butter with plastic wrap and set aside or refrigerate until ready to use. This can be made in advance and refrigerated for up to 5 days. You'll have about 16 tablespoons of shell butter, so save the extra to griddle toast, poach fish, or toss charred vegetables.

Make the paprikash: Lay the shrimp out on paper towels and season with the salt on both sides.

Melt 8 tablespoons of the shell butter and the canola oil in a large saucepan over medium-high heat. Working in batches, gently lay the shrimp down in the pan, being careful not to overcrowd. Cook on each side for 1 to 2 minutes, until the shrimp turn pink and begin to curl. Transfer to a serving platter as they finish and continue searing the rest.

Once all the shrimp are cooked, add the paprika to the saucepan and swirl vigorously for 5 seconds. Don't let the paprika sit too long on the heat or it will burn. Immediately add the white wine and use a wooden spoon to release any bits of flavor from the bottom of the pan. Simmer for about 2 minutes, until slightly reduced. Pour the pan sauce over the shrimp and serve immediately with the halved lemon. Grab plenty of napkins and dive in with your hands!

Wine pairing: Try this dish with a light bright red wine like Csókaszőlő or Portugieser.

FOR THE SHELL BUTTER

1 small yellow onion, halved

2 sticks (½ pound) unsalted butter

Shells from 2 pounds peeled jumbo shrimp

4 garlic cloves, smashed

5 fresh thyme sprigs

1 teaspoon kosher salt

FOR THE PAPRIKASH

2 pounds jumbo shrimp, peeled with tails on

1 tablespoon kosher salt

2 tablespoons canola oil

1 tablespoon smoked paprika*

½ cup dry white wine

1 lemon, halved

*For a spicy version, use hot paprika or add a pinch of cayenne pepper.

In Hungary, halászlé túrós is most associated with the holidays. It's a true peasant dish, originating with river fishers in the countryside who threw whatever they caught in the pot at the end of the day. A rich, fatty stock makes it stick to your bones and it's best served with fresh peppers, pickles, and a big chunk of bread. I actually never came across the dish until I went to Hungary. The first time I had it was in a small restaurant in Tokaj, served with the collar bone of a carp in a ruby-red stock. The best part of this stew is dunking bread to sop up the layer of paprika oil on top. The second-best part is asking for another bowl.

Serves 8 to 10

Halászlé Túrós (Fisherman's Stew)

2 tablespoons canola oil

2 large yellow onions, thinly sliced

Kosher salt

1 tablespoon tomato paste

1 cup dry white wine

1 tablespoon smoked paprika

½ tablespoon hot paprika

2 quarts high-quality fish stock (preferably homemade, page 197)

1½ pounds skin-on hake or cod fillet, cut into 2-inch chunks

2 pounds Manila clams, scrubbed

TO GARNISH

Extra-virgin olive oil

Chopped fresh dill and chives (optional)

Heat the canola oil in a large Dutch oven set over medium heat. When the oil shimmers, add the onions and a good pinch of salt. Sauté, stirring occasionally, until the onions are uniformly golden brown and starting to caramelize, 10 to 15 minutes. Be careful not to burn them. Add the tomato paste and stir until the paste begins to stick to the bottom of the pot, about 2 minutes. Deglaze with the wine and reduce until there's barely any liquid left, 5 to 7 minutes. Working quickly, add both paprikas and stir just to toast, about 5 seconds. Immediately pour in the fish stock. Bring the soup to a boil and then reduce to a low simmer. Let the soup reduce for 20 to 30 minutes, until slightly thickened and rich in flavor. Taste for seasoning and add salt as needed. With the soup simmering, carefully lower in the fish and clams. Cover and cook for about 10 minutes, stirring halfway through, until the fish is plump, opaque, and just beginning to flake. The clams should be opened. (Remove and discard any that are unopened.) Serve from the pot and garnish each bowl with a drizzle of olive oil and a sprinkle of herbs, if using.

Wine pairing: Try pairing the halászlé with a medium-bodied earthy red like Kékfrankos or Syrah.

Companions

Grandma Agi's idea of a salad was globs of dressing squeezed on iceberg lettuce. And honestly, I didn't hate it. This salad, one of the signature dishes at Agi's Counter, is a little more chef driven but keeps the spirit of abundance. I like to thickly coat sturdy leaves of escarole and radicchio in an anchovy and caraway dressing and pile them high (of course, there's plenty of dill mixed in with the leaves). The bread crumbs are an imitation of the seasoned Vigo bread crumbs my mom always loved to use. And finally, the salad gets blanketed in finely shaved Parmesan to complete my ideal trifecta.

Serves 4

Caraway Caesar Salad

FOR THE DRESSING

4 anchovy fillets

3 large egg yolks

3 garlic cloves

¼ cup champagne vinegar

2 tablespoons caraway seeds, ground

1 tablespoon Dijon mustard

A few ice cubes

1½ cups canola oil

FOR THE BREAD CRUMBS

2 cups plain bread crumbs, store-bought or homemade

½ tablespoon dried parsley

½ tablespoon dried oregano

1 teaspoon garlic powder

1 teaspoon kosher salt

2 tablespoons extra-virgin olive oil

Make the dressing: Combine the anchovies, egg yolks, garlic, vinegar, caraway, mustard, and ice in a blender. Blend on high speed just until the garlic and anchovies are broken down, about 10 seconds. With the blender running on high speed, slowly add the canola oil in a steady stream until the dressing comes together. It should be slightly thick. Transfer to an airtight container and refrigerate until ready to use. This makes 2 cups (bonus dressing!) so store leftovers in the refrigerator for up to 5 days.

Make the bread crumbs: Preheat the oven to 350°F. Line a rimmed baking sheet with parchment paper.

Toss together the bread crumbs, parsley, oregano, garlic powder, salt, and olive oil in a large bowl until combined. Spread the bread crumbs evenly on the prepared baking sheet. Toast until golden brown, about 10 minutes, stirring halfway through to ensure even color. Set aside to cool completely. I like to make extra of these to have on hand, so this makes more than you need. Store any extra bread crumbs in an airtight container at room temperature for up to 2 weeks.

Assemble the salad: Have a serving platter or large salad bowl ready. Combine the escarole, radicchio, dill, 1 cup of the cheese, the olive oil, lemon juice, pepper, and 1 cup of the dressing in a large bowl. Using your clean hands (yes, this gets messy), toss together the ingredients, massaging the leaves so the dressing gets in all the nooks and crannies.

RECIPE CONTINUES

FOR THE SALAD

2 heads of escarole, cleaned and pulled apart into whole leaves

1 head of radicchio, cleaned and pulled apart into whole leaves

1 bunch of fresh dill, roughly chopped

6 ounces Grana Padano or Parmesan, grated (1½ cups)

¼ cup extra-virgin olive oil, plus more to garnish

Juice of 1 lemon

1 teaspoon freshly ground black pepper

Transfer the salad to the platter, piling it high to achieve a dramatic look. Rinse and dry your hands. Sprinkle 1 cup of the bread crumbs over the salad as well as the remaining ½ cup cheese. Finish with a final drizzle of olive oil.

A Messy Herby Potato Salad (page 110),
Beans with Poppy Seeds, Pine Nuts &
Fennel (page 109), and Agi's Counter
Cabbage Slaw (page 108)

A big part of being Jewish is the weekly (or sometimes daily) pilgrimage to the deli to stock up on sides and the latest gossip. That deli counter culture has forever had a huge influence on me, in my restaurant and in this book, so the following three recipes are my homage to my childhood favorites.

This punchy cabbage slaw is the signature slaw we serve at Agi's Counter. It's always nestled alongside sandwiches or dense mains that need something refreshing. I believe the best slaws are messy, saucy, and leave mayo on the sides of your mouth. This one hits a delicate balance of fatty mayo and acidic vinegar for a slaw that's light and satisfying but still just a little bit messy.

When it comes to bean salads, all my memories are from the summers at Nana Arlene's North Carolina beach house, where she would get containers for lunch from the local deli. This version really scratches the itch for a great salad. The beans are simmered in a rich stock so they're plump with flavor. Then they get tossed with pine nuts toasted in browned butter, crunchy poppy seeds, and the fresh anise bite of fennel fronds.

And I love all potato salads, but my favorites are heavy on flavor while still feeling light and fresh. This one accomplishes all that with an herb-packed dressing that highlights the potato. Tossing it with the still-hot potatoes lets them soak in the oil and lemon juice, flavoring them from the inside out. Just like the other two, it's a big, beautiful salad, without feeling overly heavy and dense.

Serves 4

Agi's Counter Cabbage Slaw

1 medium head of purple cabbage (green or a combo is also fine), cored and thinly sliced

½ medium red onion, thinly sliced

1 tablespoon dill seeds

3 tablespoons rice wine vinegar

3 tablespoons Kewpie mayonnaise or Schmaltz Mayo (page 193)

½ cup chopped fresh dill

Kosher salt and freshly ground black pepper

Toss together all the ingredients in a large bowl until thoroughly combined. Marinate in the refrigerator for at least 1 hour before serving or store in an airtight container in the refrigerator for up to 24 hours.

Beans with Poppy Seeds, Pine Nuts & Fennel

Make the beans: Heat the canola oil in a medium heavy-bottomed saucepan over medium-low heat. When the oil shimmers, add the carrot, celery, onion, and fennel bulb. Lightly salt the vegetables and cook, stirring occasionally, until they're starting to become translucent, about 6 minutes. Add the garlic and stir for 2 minutes. Add the beans, stock, and bay leaves. Bring to a boil, then quickly reduce the heat to low. Cover the saucepan and simmer the beans for 45 minutes to 1 hour. Check on them periodically for tenderness. They should be soft but with a little bite. Remove from the heat and let cool completely in the liquid, about 1 hour.

Make the salad: Combine the pine nuts and butter in a medium skillet over medium heat and let the butter melt and the nuts toast, stirring occasionally, until the nuts are golden brown and the butter is foaming and brown, 6 to 8 minutes. Remove from the heat. Set a fine-mesh strainer over a small bowl. Strain the nuts, reserving the browned butter in an airtight container for future uses. (Store the butter in the refrigerator for up to 5 days.) Let the nuts cool completely.

Drain the cooled beans, but save ½ cup of cooking liquid.* Combine the beans with the reserved fennel fronds, toasted pine nuts, poppy seeds, scallions, olive oil, and vinegar in a large bowl. Season to taste with salt and pepper. Toss thoroughly to combine. Stir in the reserved ½ cup cooking liquid. Taste the seasoning before serving and adjust if needed.

*Freeze the remaining bean liquid in an airtight container for up to 3 months. It's perfect for building a great base for soups!

FOR THE BEANS

2 tablespoons canola oil

1 large carrot, cut into large chunks

2 celery stalks, cut into large chunks

1 medium yellow onion, quartered

1 medium fennel bulb, fronds reserved, quartered

Kosher salt

3 garlic cloves, smashed

½ pound navy beans, rinsed and drained (preferably Alubia Blanca from Rancho Gordo)

4 cups vegetable or chicken stock, store-bought or homemade (page 196)

2 dried bay leaves

FOR THE SALAD

1 cup pine nuts

1 stick (8 tablespoons) unsalted butter

1 tablespoon poppy seeds

1 cup thinly sliced scallions

½ cup extra-virgin olive oil

¼ cup champagne vinegar or Chamomile Vinegar (page 194)

Kosher salt and freshly ground black pepper

A Messy Herby Potato Salad

2 pounds multicolor marble potatoes or any small waxy potatoes

Kosher salt

¼ cup extra-virgin olive oil

¼ cup canola oil

½ cup chopped fresh parsley leaves, plus more to garnish

½ cup chopped fresh dill, plus more to garnish

½ cup chopped fresh mint leaves, plus more to garnish

4 anchovy fillets

3 tablespoons fresh lemon juice

¼ cup minced fresh chives

Arrange the potatoes in a medium saucepan and cover with water. Aggressively season the water with a few big pinches of salt. Set over high heat, bring to a boil, and cook for about 20 minutes, until the potatoes are fork-tender. Drain and cool.

While the potatoes are cooking, make the dressing. Combine the olive oil, canola oil, parsley, dill, mint, and anchovies in a blender or food processor. Blend for about 1 minute, until the oil turns emerald green. (Alternatively, you can finely chop the herbs and anchovy and fold into the oil.)

When the potatoes are still warm but cool enough to handle, slice them in half and transfer to a large bowl. Toss the potatoes with the dressing and lemon juice. Taste for seasoning and adjust if needed. Garnish with the minced chives and remaining herbs before serving.

This is a fan favorite side that's almost always on the menu at Agi's Counter. It started as an homage to Grandma Agi and her bottle of ranch that was omnipresent at the table. Agi never met a green vegetable that didn't need a swipe through her trusty dressing. This homemade ranch is a little more tangy and punchy with lots of lemon (Meyer lemons work beautifully here) and sits thickly on the cucumbers. The addition of horseradish gives it a nice zing that pulls it back from getting too rich. Serve these cucumbers cold alongside anything fried or fatty that needs a refreshing balance.

Serves 4

Cucumber & Buttermilk Ranch

Cut the cucumbers into quarters lengthwise, then cut each strip in half on the bias to make 2 jagged spears. Toss the cucumbers with 1 teaspoon salt in a large bowl and let them "cure" for 30 minutes.

Meanwhile, in a medium bowl, whisk together the sour cream, buttermilk, mustard powder, garlic powder, parsley, and lemon zest. Season to taste with salt and pepper. Add the dressing and the lemon juice to the bowl with the cucumbers and toss to coat. Arrange on a serving platter and sprinkle the grated horseradish on top.

½ pound Persian cucumbers

Kosher salt

1 cup sour cream

½ cup plus 2 tablespoons full-fat buttermilk

1½ teaspoons mustard powder

1½ teaspoons garlic powder

1½ teaspoons dried parsley

Zest of 1 lemon

Freshly ground black pepper

Juice of 1 lemon

½ cup freshly grated horseradish, plus more as needed ('cause more is better)

My deep love for tomatoes and feta is a bit of a miracle considering my mom and dad do not like them. Instead, it was Nana Arlene who got the combo stuck in my head. (Nana Arlene is Sephardic, so feta runs in her veins.) I would sometimes get to accompany her to the country club for lunch, served buffet-style, where she arranged wedges of tomatoes and cubes of feta alongside piles of sliced vegetables and let me pick off her plate. This take on a Greek salad is so simple, but each element is considered, so make sure to invest in good ingredients. And while some precise knife work makes this salad composed enough for the country club set, it's still loose enough for Arlene's plate.

Serves 4 to 6

A Greek Salad

2 pounds tomatoes,* halved or quartered depending on size

1 medium red onion, sliced into thin rounds

1 large cucumber, peeled and sliced into thin rounds

1 green bell pepper, core and seeds removed, sliced into thin rings

2 tablespoons white balsamic vinegar

1 teaspoon kosher salt

12 ounces feta (Bulgarian or goat's-milk feta are great options), sliced into slabs

1 cup pitted kalamata olives, split

½ cup fresh dill, roughly chopped

TO GARNISH

Extra-virgin olive oil

Dried oregano

Flaky sea salt

In a large bowl, combine the tomato, onion, cucumber, and bell pepper. Gently toss with the vinegar and salt. Set aside for 30 minutes at room temperature to marinate.

Transfer the mixture to a serving platter with all the juices that have accumulated. Top with the sliced feta, olives, and dill. Garnish with a good drizzle of olive oil and a sprinkle of dried oregano and flaky salt.

*This recipe relies on in-season tomatoes that are juicy, plump, colorful, and ripe to the point that they're almost bursting.

This dish pushes sweet ingredients in a savory direction while taking the savory in a sweet direction. Mostly, it's an incredible way to highlight peak-season stone fruit, which gets marinated in a fragrant, floral dressing and pairs beautifully with the creamy, tangy goat cheese. It's my ultimate dish for al fresco summer dining.

Serves 4

Peaches & Cream

Toss the fruit with the vinegar and olive oil in a large bowl. Set aside to marinate.

Meanwhile, toast the fennel seeds in a small dry sauté pan over medium heat until just fragrant, about 3 minutes. Pull off the heat immediately and add the canola oil to the pan, swirling to mix with the seeds. Pour the fennel oil over the marinating stone fruit and stir to combine. Cover and let sit for 30 minutes or up to 1 hour* at room temperature.

Cut the goat cheese log into ¼-inch rounds and arrange over a large serving plate. Spoon the stone fruit evenly over the goat cheese and make sure to flood the plate with the fennel oil. Garnish with a small pinch of flaky salt and the basil and, if using, the red currants, anise hyssop, and/or lemon balm.

*Softer, riper fruit should sit no more than 30 minutes; firmer fruit is improved with a longer soak.

8 mixed ripe stone fruits, such as peaches, plums, and nectarines, pitted and quartered

2 tablespoons white balsamic vinegar

¼ cup extra-virgin olive oil

1 tablespoon fennel seeds

¼ cup canola oil

4 ounces plain goat cheese (preferably in a log form)

TO GARNISH

Flaky sea salt

Fresh basil leaves

A few fresh red currants (optional)

Anise hyssop flowers and leaves (optional)

Lemon balm leaves (optional)

These beets—an essential ingredient in Hungarian and Jewish cooking—used to be on my menus at the Eddy and Wallflower, but I had already been making them for myself for a long time. When I started dating my boyfriend, Michael, this was one of the first things I made him and it turned him from beet avoidant into a beet lover. The tender beets get smashed, like a broken heart, then marinated in a sweet-savory mix of garlic honey, olive oil, and vinegar so the flavors can seep into all the cracks and crevices. The blue cheese is optional, but it really balances all the flavors and adds a nice creaminess.

Serves 4

Heartbroken Beets

2 pounds small red beets

½ cup Fermented Garlic Honey (page 195) or wildflower honey

2 cups extra-virgin olive oil

1 cup white balsamic vinegar

Kosher salt

5 ounces blue cheese, sliced into thin shards (optional)

Place the beets in a large pot of water and bring to a boil over high heat. Cook for about 45 minutes, until fork-tender. Drain the beets and cool slightly until just cool enough to handle. Using a rag, wipe the skins off the beets. Discard the skins. Place the beets on a cutting board and gently press the beets using the palm of your hand just until they split open. Transfer the beets to an airtight container.

Whisk together the garlic honey, olive oil, vinegar, and a generous pinch of salt in a large bowl. Pour the dressing over the beets so they are completely covered. Let the beets marinate for as long as possible, up to 1 day at room temperature or up to 2 weeks in the refrigerator.

Spoon the beets onto a serving plate. The marinade should leach out onto the plate and pool around the beets. Scatter the shards of blue cheese around the beets.

Radishes and eggs make me think of every event at Jewish temple with a spread of sliced, watery, generic radishes and hard-boiled eggs. Even at my Jewish day school, we often had hard-boiled eggs and radishes for lunch. So that flavor profile has really stuck with me, maybe even haunted me. This version treats everything with a little more care, for something that's deeply satisfying. Poaching the radishes helps mellow their spicy bite and gives them an almost meaty tenderness. I'm a big supporter of soft-boiling eggs always, letting the jammy yolk be the center of richness. And finally, a few spoonfuls of roe add a perfect salty brine to balance it all out.

Serves 4

Poached Radishes

Toss the radishes with the kosher salt in a large bowl. Set aside to "cure" for up to 1 hour at room temperature.

Bring the butter and stock to a simmer in a large saucepan over low heat. Add the radishes to the pan in a single even layer. Cook for about 5 minutes, until the radishes begin to turn translucent. Spoon the radishes from the pan onto a serving platter or into a large bowl.

Peel and quarter the soft-boiled eggs. Garnish with the quartered eggs and dollops of smoked trout roe. Finish with a sprinkle of flaky salt.

1 pound red breakfast radishes, stems removed, halved or quartered depending on size

1 teaspoon kosher salt

6 tablespoons unsalted butter

½ cup vegetable or chicken stock, store-bought or homemade (page 196)

2 large eggs, boiled for 6 minutes and cooled (see "On Boiling Eggs," page 14)

2 ounces smoked trout roe

Flaky sea salt, to garnish

Stuffed is sort of the only right answer for what to do with squash blossoms. Instead of the typical ricotta filling, I like to lean into the creamy texture and savory flavor of körözött, Hungary's answer to pimento cheese. Filling and frying the blossoms is a great communal project and gets easier and easier once you have your method down. When these are hot and crispy, they are incredibly addictive, and I've been known to eat an entire tray by myself. Just be warned: The filling is molten lava when they come out of the oil.

Makes 2 dozen stuffed blossoms

Körözött-Stuffed Squash Blossoms

Pour enough oil (likely about 2 quarts) into a large Dutch oven to reach a depth of 2 inches. Set over medium-high heat and bring to a temperature of 375°F on a deep-fry thermometer. While the oil is heating, set yourself up with a rimmed baking sheet lined with paper towels and/or a cooling rack. You'll also need a wide slotted spoon or spider strainer.

Fill a piping bag or plastic zip-top bag with the körözött. Snip off the end. Pipe about 1 tablespoon of filling into each blossom. The filling should just meet where the petals begin to separate. Twist the tips of the petals to lock in the filling. Repeat with the remaining blossoms.

Make the batter: Whisk together the flour and cornstarch in a large bowl. Add the club soda and whisk until the batter is smooth and runny.

Working in batches, pick up 1 blossom at a time by its stem and dip into the batter. Carefully lower into the frying oil, then repeat with a few more blossoms. Don't crowd the surface. Fry for about 2 minutes per side, until lightly golden brown. Remove from the oil with a slotted spoon and set on the paper towels or rack to drain. Repeat with the remaining blossoms in batches, making sure the oil maintains a temperature of 375°F. Sprinkle the fried blossoms with salt and let cool just slightly before serving.

Canola oil, for frying

2 cups Körözött (page 20)

24 squash blossoms, stamen removed

Kosher salt

FOR THE BATTER

1⅔ cups all-purpose flour

1½ cups cornstarch

3½ cups cold club soda

This dish is so deeply in the pocket of fall comfort, and I love the carrot-on-carrot action. It's a little unusual to have a creamy carrot puree lying underneath roasted carrots, but the combo really hits home for me, especially with floral sage and a rich and fatty vinaigrette. Speck, a cured pork cut, adds a ton of smoky umami flavor that compliments the naturally sweet carrots. (Bacon works great too.) A drizzle of fermented garlic honey is the perfect final touch to mimic the sweet-savory play of the other ingredients.

Serves 4

Carrots & Crispy Speck

FOR THE PUREE

1 pound carrots, cut into ½-inch pieces

½ teaspoon kosher salt

1 tablespoon unsalted butter

FOR THE ROASTED CARROTS

1 pound carrots

2 tablespoons extra-virgin olive oil

½ teaspoon kosher salt

½ teaspoon freshly ground black pepper

4 tablespoons canola oil

4 ounces speck, torn into 1-inch pieces

½ cup fresh sage leaves

Juice of 1 lemon

TO GARNISH

1 tablespoon Fermented Garlic Honey (page 195)

Flaky sea salt

Preheat the oven to 400°F.

Make the puree: In a small saucepan, combine the carrots, salt, and 1 tablespoon of water. Cover and set over medium-low heat. Simmer, stirring occasionally, until the carrots are tender but not taking on any color, about 20 minutes. Transfer to a blender with the butter and blend until smooth. Set aside to cool to room temperature.

Make the roasted carrots: Cut the carrots in half crosswise, then cut each piece in half lengthwise. On a rimmed baking sheet, toss the carrots, olive oil, salt, and pepper. Roast for about 15 minutes, until golden brown and crisp-tender. Set aside to cool.

In a large saute pan, heat 1 tablespoon of canola oil over medium-high heat. When the oil shimmers, add the speck and use a wooden spoon to stir it as it crisps, about 5 minutes. Transfer to paper towels to drain. Add the remaining 3 tablespoons of canola oil and reduce the heat to low. Add the sage (the oil will splatter, so be careful) and shake the pan as the sage fries, no more than 2 minutes. Remove the sage to the same paper towels to drain. Pour the fragrant oil into a medium bowl and cool for 15 minutes, then vigorously whisk in the lemon juice to emulsify.

On a large serving platter, dollop the puree in the center and spread around slightly to create a well. Arrange the roasted carrots with the fried speck and sage, weaving into layers. Drizzle the oil mixture on top, then finish with the garlic honey and a pinch of flaky salt.

This is Grandma Agi's idea of a vegetable side. Despite its plain name, it's actually the richest possible version of cauliflower, loaded with butter, sour cream, and cheese. Because of everything going on here, I grew up loving cauliflower way before it was cool to love cauliflower. (Because of everything going on here, it's debatable if I even understood what cauliflower tasted like.) Agi would bring it to the table in a white floral serving dish, covered in pools of oil. This version is slightly lighter than Agi's but stays true to the deep comfort of her signature side dish.

Serves 4

Cauliflower Mush

Fill a large pot with 4 cups water and bring to a simmer over medium-high heat. Set a colander or mesh strainer over the pot. Place the cauliflower in the colander and cover the pot with a lid. If it won't close all the way, lay a piece of aluminum foil between the colander and the lid to create a tight seal. Steam the cauliflower until fork-tender, about 15 minutes. Transfer the steamed cauliflower to a food processor.

Meanwhile, melt the butter in a small sauté pan over medium heat. Add the garlic and stir frequently until fragrant and starting to toast, about 2 minutes. Transfer the garlic and butter to the food processor. Blend until the cauliflower is mostly smooth with a few chunks. Transfer the cauliflower mush to a medium bowl. Use a rubber spatula to fold in the Grana Padano, sour cream, salt, and 1 teaspoon pepper. Taste for seasoning and adjust if needed.

Mound the mush on a serving platter and create dramatic swirls using the back of a spoon. Drizzle with olive oil, letting it pool in places, and finish with an extra sprinkle of pepper.

1 medium head of cauliflower, cut into florets

3 tablespoons unsalted butter

3 garlic cloves, minced

¼ cup Grana Padano

¼ cup sour cream

½ tablespoon kosher salt, plus more as needed

1 teaspoon freshly ground black pepper, plus more

Extra-virgin olive oil

In Hungary, cakes are not a dessert, they're an all-day snack, with cafes solely dedicated to delicately layered confections. Instead of ending your day, they're meant to pause your day while you catch up with a friend or have a quiet moment to relax

Cakes & Tortes

Rigó Jancsi Torte (page 139),
Gerbeaud (page 134), and
Bay Leaf Cream Slice (page 137)

Gerbeaud is the Betty Crocker of Hungarian cakes: it's a household name and everyone loves it. In the 1800s, Swiss-born Emil Gerbeaud moved to Budapest and opened his eponymous cafe and patisserie, where this cake was born. (In the 1900s, Grandma Agi would go to the cafe after school for an espresso and slice of cake.) Hungarian desserts usually involve some combination of nuts, jam, and chocolate, and this cake is kind of the epitome. It takes a little TLC to assemble, but it's worth the effort for a cake that's airy and lightly sweet.

Makes 20 pieces

Gerbeaud

1½ cups whole milk, slightly warm

1½ tablespoons active dry yeast

8⅔ cups all-purpose flour

2 tablespoons baking powder

1¼ cups sugar

4 sticks (1 pound) unsalted butter, room temperature

3 large eggs

½ cup apricot jam

1 cup walnuts, finely chopped

6 ounces bittersweet chocolate (64%), chopped

½ cup heavy cream

1 tablespoon corn syrup

Whisk together the warm milk and yeast in a small bowl. Let stand for about 5 minutes, until foamy and fragrant. In the bowl of a stand mixer fitted with the paddle attachment, mix the flour, baking powder, sugar, and butter to make a sandy mixture. Add the yeast mixture and eggs to the flour mixture. Beat until it just comes together, 2 to 3 minutes. Turn out the dough and separate into 3 equal pieces. Cover each piece tightly with plastic wrap and refrigerate for 30 minutes to rest.

Preheat the oven to 350°F.

Lay out two 13 × 18-inch pieces of parchment. Set 1 piece of dough between the parchment pieces and roll until you have a large rectangle that reaches the edges of the parchment. Repeat with more parchment and the remaining dough.

Place 1 layer of dough on a 13 × 18-inch rimmed baking sheet. Peel away the top layer of parchment. Spread ¼ cup of the apricot jam evenly over the whole surface. Sprinkle with ½ cup of the walnuts. Remove the top layer of parchment from the second sheet of dough and flip the dough onto the first layer. Peel away the remaining parchment. Spread the remaining ¼ cup apricot jam over the dough and sprinkle with the remaining ½ cup walnuts. Remove the top layer of parchment from the remaining layer of dough and flip the dough on top, then remove the remaining parchment. Bake for about 20 minutes, rotating halfway through, until the top is golden brown. Let cool completely on the baking sheet.

RECIPE CONTINUES

Gerbeaud (page 134),
Rigó Jancsi Torte (page 139), and
Bay Leaf Cream Slice (page 137)

When the cake has cooled, put the chocolate in a medium heatproof bowl. Bring the heavy cream and corn syrup to a boil in a small saucepan over medium heat. Pour over the chocolate. Let sit for 1 minute, then whisk until smooth. Pour the ganache over the top of the cake in an even layer. Use an offset spatula to smooth as needed. Refrigerate the cake until the chocolate is set, at least 2 hours or up to 24 hours before serving.

Trim the sides of the cake for clean slices. I like to lightly press my knife onto the ganache to mark the cake before cutting. We're going for 20 pieces here, so mark off 3 lines by 4 lines on the chocolate surface to make a 4 × 5 grid. For the cleanest cut, run a knife under hot water, then wipe it dry. Cut along the lines, wiping and rewarming the knife after each cut.

Cover and store any leftovers in the refrigerator for up to 1 week. Bring to room temperature for about an hour before serving. The cake can also be wrapped tightly and frozen for up to 2 months. Defrost in the refrigerator overnight.

In every Hungarian bakery refrigerator, you'll find krémes. It's a simple dessert, just two pieces of puff pastry sandwiching a thick layer of pastry cream and cut into massive cubes. This version is slightly different, with a thinner, more manageable layer of cream infused with floral, piney notes of bay leaves. It's a very simple cake, but that's the beauty of it. Buttery, flaky pastry plus velvety smooth custard. You don't need anything else. My final touch is dusting the confectioners' sugar over a few bay leaves to leave a silhouette on the surface. It's a small detail that makes for a showstopping piece to serve at the table.

Serves 8 to 10

Bay Leaf Cream Slice

Make the pastry cream: Prepare an ice-water bath in a large bowl. Set aside.

Heat the milk, vanilla bean (seeds and pod), and bay leaves in a small saucepan over medium heat until the milk just begins to steam, about 3 minutes. Remove from the heat and cover with a lid. Let the mixture steep at room temperature for at least 1 hour or up to 2 hours. Fish out the bay leaves and vanilla pod. Save the bay leaves by drying them on a set of paper towels (you will need them to garnish).

Whisk together the egg yolks, granulated sugar, cornstarch, and a pinch of salt in a large bowl to make a thick pale yellow mixture. Set the milk back over medium heat briefly until it just begins to steam again. While whisking constantly, stream the warm milk into the egg mixture. Pour the mixture back into the saucepan and set back over medium heat. Whisk the mixture continuously (don't step away!) until it has thickened, about 5 minutes. Remove from the heat and whisk in the butter until melted and combined. Immediately transfer the pastry cream to a medium bowl and set in the ice-water bath. Press plastic wrap directly on the surface of the custard to stop a skin from forming. Chill the custard for 30 minutes in the bath, then remove the bowl and continue to chill for 2 hours in the refrigerator.

Make the cake: Line two large rimmed baking sheets with parchment paper. Arrange 1 sheet of puff pastry on each prepared baking sheet and bake according to the package instructions. Let cool completely before assembling. Spread or pipe the pastry cream in an even layer

FOR THE PASTRY CREAM
4 cups whole milk

2 vanilla beans, halved lengthwise and seeds scraped

24 dried bay leaves

8 large egg yolks

1 cup granulated sugar

6 tablespoons cornstarch

Kosher salt

4 tablespoons unsalted butter, cut into small pieces

FOR THE CAKE
2 sheets store-bought puff pastry, thawed

Confectioners' sugar, to garnish

RECIPE CONTINUES

on 1 sheet of puff pastry, leaving a 1-inch border around the edge. Top with the second sheet of pastry and transfer to the fridge to set for 1 hour.

When ready to serve, arrange the dried bay leaves on top of the pastry in a scattered pattern. Liberally dust the pastry with confectioners' sugar until the entire surface is covered. Using a pair of tweezers or your fingers, carefully lift the bay leaves off the top, leaving behind silhouettes. Run a knife under hot water, then wipe it dry before slicing the cake. The puff pastry will make for flaky, messy slices, but that's the pleasure of this cake. Cream Slice is best enjoyed the same day.

This torte is named after a famous Hungarian violinist, Rigó Jancsi, and has a very dramatic backstory. While Jancsi was playing with his orchestra in a Paris restaurant, he caught the attention of Clara Ward, who was the daughter of an American millionaire and the wife of a Belgian prince. He seduced and eventually married her, causing a massive scandal and decades of gossip. This cake is just as seductive, with thin layers of chocolate cake sandwiching chocolate mousse and covered in chocolate glaze. It's decadent, romantic, and easy to love.

Serves 6 to 8

Rigó Jancsi Torte

Make the cake: Preheat the oven to 350°F. Grease a large rimmed baking sheet (roughly 13 × 18 × 1 inch) with a little butter. Line with parchment paper and grease again.

In the bowl of a stand mixer fitted with the whisk attachment, beat the egg yolks with ¼ cup of the sugar on medium speed until the mixture is thick, pale, and ribbon-like, about 5 minutes. Transfer the yolk mixture to a large bowl. Wash and dry the mixer bowl and whisk, then return to the stand mixer. Beat the egg whites with a big pinch of salt on medium speed until foamy, about 1 minute. Gradually pour in the remaining ¼ cup sugar and continue mixing until the egg whites reach stiff peaks, about 3 minutes.

Place the chopped chocolate in a small bowl, then pour the boiling water over the chocolate. Let sit for 1 minute, then whisk until smooth. Fold the melted chocolate into the yolk mixture. Scoop ¼ cup of the whipped egg whites into the bowl with the yolk mixture and fold to combine. Sift in the flour and gently fold, then the remaining egg whites. Pour the batter onto the prepared baking sheet and use a wet spatula to smooth into an even layer. Bake for 15 to 20 minutes, until a toothpick inserted in the center comes out clean. This cake won't really rise so don't be alarmed! Let cool completely. Use the parchment to slide the cake onto a cutting board. Trim all the edges of the cake, then cut the cake in half across the width. Brush the surface with rum.

Make the mousse: Combine the chocolate and butter in a medium bowl. Bring the heavy cream and corn syrup to a boil in a small

RECIPE CONTINUES

FOR THE CAKE

Unsalted butter, for greasing

6 large eggs, separated

½ cup sugar

Kosher salt

6 ounces bittersweet chocolate (64%), chopped

¼ cup boiling water

¼ cup all-purpose flour

2 tablespoons light rum

FOR THE MOUSSE

16 ounces bittersweet chocolate (64%), chopped

2 tablespoons unsalted butter

1½ cups heavy cream

2 tablespoons corn syrup

FOR THE GLAZE

6 ounces bittersweet chocolate (64%), chopped

½ cup heavy cream

2 tablespoons corn syrup

TO GARNISH

¼ cup cocoa powder

Flaky sea salt

saucepan over medium heat. Pour the mixture over the chocolate and butter. Let sit for 1 minute, then whisk until smooth. Refrigerate the mixture for about 30 minutes until it's slightly warm, about 80°F. Either by hand or using an electric mixer, whip the chocolate mixture until light and fluffy.

To assemble the cake, reserve one-quarter of the mousse. Spread the rest evenly over one of the layers of cake, leaving a ½-inch border on all sides. Set the other half of the cake on top of the mousse and press gently. Use the remaining mousse to fill in the gaps all the way around the cake (it should resemble an ice-cream sandwich).

Make the glaze: Place the chocolate in a medium bowl. In a small saucepan over medium heat, bring the heavy cream and corn syrup to a boil. Pour the mixture over the chocolate. Let sit for 1 minute, then whisk until smooth. Spread the glaze over the top of the cake in an even layer. Freeze the cake for 30 minutes until everything is set.

Before serving, garnish the top of the cake with a dusting of cocoa powder and a sprinkle of flaky salt. Run a knife under hot water, then wipe it dry. Cut the cake into large squares or diamonds, wiping and rewarming the knife after each cut.

Cover and store any leftovers in the refrigerator for up to 1 week. Bring to room temperature for about an hour before serving. The cake can also be wrapped tightly and frozen for up to 2 months. Defrost in the refrigerator overnight.

Many people don't realize that the popular internet recipe for monkey bread originated as the Hungarian arany galuska, or golden dumpling. Traditionally this pull-apart cake is made with a bunch of small and overly sweet balls, but I wanted this version to embrace a larger scale with a bunch of fluffy, slightly sweet rolls spiked with cardamom. Since the rolls are less sweet, the crème anglaise, a vanilla–heavy cream sauce, is served on the side for dunking. I love having this cake for breakfast with coffee, but it's great any time of day. The only important rule is you have to eat it straight out of the oven while it's still warm and very fragrant!

Serves 10

Golden Dumpling Cake

Make the cake: Heat the milk in a small saucepan over low heat until warm to the touch. Transfer to a small bowl and add the yeast and ¼ teaspoon of the sugar. Stir and let sit at room temperature until the yeast has bloomed or started to foam, about 5 minutes. In the bowl of a stand mixer fitted with the hook attachment, combine the remaining 3 tablespoons sugar with the flour, eggs, cardamom, rum, vanilla seeds, and the milk mixture. Mix on medium speed until a smooth ball forms. Add 3 tablespoons of the melted butter, a tablespoon at a time, mixing completely after each addition. Turn out the dough onto a lightly floured surface and knead by hand for 5 minutes, until soft and not sticky. Place the dough back in the bowl, cover with plastic wrap, and set somewhere warm to proof until doubled in size, about 1 hour. (Near the oven is always a good spot to get ambient heat.)

Preheat the oven to 350°F. Brush an 8-inch round cake pan with a little melted butter.

Tear a golf ball–size piece of the dough and roll into a ball. Repeat with the remaining dough for about 10 balls. Pour the remaining melted butter into a small bowl and dunk each ball into the butter. Arrange the dough balls in the prepared pan so they all fit together nice and snug. Bake for 20 to 30 minutes. The cake should be tall and golden brown. Remove from the oven. Set a wire rack over the cake and invert the pan to release. Set a serving platter over the bottom of the cake and invert again so it's right side up.

FOR THE CAKE

½ cup whole milk

2¼ teaspoons active dry yeast (from a ¼-ounce packet)

3 tablespoons plus ¼ teaspoon sugar

2⅔ cups all-purpose flour, plus more as needed

2 large eggs

1 tablespoon ground cardamom

1 tablespoon rum

1 vanilla bean, halved lengthwise and seeds scraped

2 sticks (½ pound) plus 3 tablespoons unsalted butter, melted, plus more for the pan

FOR THE SAUCE

4 large egg yolks

¼ cup sugar

½ cup whole milk

½ cup heavy cream

RECIPE CONTINUES

½ teaspoon pure vanilla extract

¼ teaspoon orange blossom water

While the cake bakes, make the sauce: Whisk together the egg yolks and sugar to make a thick, pale yellow mixture in a medium bowl. In a medium saucepan, combine the milk and heavy cream. Set over medium heat and bring to a gentle simmer, then remove from the heat. While whisking constantly, stream the warm milk mixture into the egg mixture. Pour the mixture back into the saucepan and set back over medium heat. Stir the mixture continuously with a wooden spoon until the sauce thickens and coats the back of the spoon, about 5 minutes. Remove from the heat and whisk in the vanilla extract and the orange blossom water. Pour the sauce through a fine-mesh strainer into a gravy boat or small pitcher. Serve warm alongside the cake. Golden Dumpling demands to be eaten immediately.

This pancake torte was inspired by George Lang, a Hungarian restaurateur in New York. His book, *The Cuisine of Hungary*, was very important to me, and it had a recipe for this pancake torte. It's basically a crepe cake, but instead of thick layers of whipped cream, the crepes are layered with thinly spread jam (very Hungarian to pick jam over cream). It takes a little work, but it's a great assembly-line project with family or friends plus a few bottles of wine. The final touch is a chocolate sauce spiked with rum, for a perfect balance between fancy and casual.

Serves 8

Pancake Torte

Set a small station up around your stove. You'll need:
- Softened unsalted butter with a small spoon
- A 2-ounce ladle or ¼-cup measure
- A rubber spatula
- A large plate for finished crepes

Make the crepes: Whisk together the flour, milk, seltzer, eggs, vanilla, and a big pinch of salt in a large bowl. Let the batter rest in the refrigerator for 30 minutes to set.

Set an 8-inch crepe pan or nonstick skillet over medium-high heat. Add a small scoop of butter to the pan, tilting to cover the surface. Ladle the crepe batter onto the pan, tilting so the batter covers the entire surface. Don't be afraid to add a little more batter if it needs it. Let the first side of the crepe cook for about 2 minutes. You'll know to flip when the sides of the crepe begin to peel up off the pan. Using a spatula, flip the crepe over and continue to cook on the other side for less than a minute. The result should be a golden-brown crepe that looks like it has craters spattered about it. Your first crepe will most likely be a throwaway and that's normal. Every batch should get a practice run. Continue with the rest of the batter to make 8 crepes, stacking each one on the plate as they're done.

To assemble the cake: Lay 1 crepe in the center of a large serving plate. Spread 2 tablespoons of jam evenly across the surface. Place another crepe directly over the first one and repeat, using all the crepes. Keep the final layer clear on top.

Cut the cake into 8 wedges. Serve your guests with a gravy boat or small pitcher of warm chocolate rum sauce and a small bowl of chopped pistachios to garnish. Pancake Torte is best enjoyed the same day.

FOR THE CREPES

2 cups all-purpose flour

2 cups whole milk

¾ cup plus 2 tablespoons cold seltzer

4 large eggs

1 tablespoon pure vanilla extract

Kosher salt

Unsalted butter, for greasing

TO ASSEMBLE

1½ cups jam, room temperature (raspberry, apricot, or orange are all great)

Chocolate Rum Sauce (page 203)

1 cup pistachios, toasted and chopped (see page 209)

The words *coffee cake* immediately send my mind to my favorite, which is Entenmann's. Nana Arlene's husband, Papa Howie, owned a pharmacy and they stocked the full line of Entenmann's products. But I had eyes only for that coffee cake and couldn't wait to get home, open the box, and dive in with a fork. The addition of prunes here was also inspired by the pharmacy: the cakes were right across from the prune juice. I am a big prune advocate and I'm not afraid to say it. They get a bad rap as old-people food, but they're so delicious. This recipe was developed by Agi Counter's original pastry chef, Renee Hudson, and it captures so many memories in every slice.

Serves 8

Prune Coffee Cake

FOR THE PRUNES

2 cups pitted prunes, quartered

3 fresh bay leaves

1 strip of lemon peel

1 strip of orange peel

3 cardamom pods, smashed

1 cinnamon stick

¼ cup brandy

FOR THE STREUSEL

1 cup rye flour

¼ cup granulated sugar

¼ cup packed dark brown sugar

6 tablespoons unsalted butter, room temperature

½ teaspoon kosher salt

½ teaspoon ground cinnamon

½ teaspoon ground cardamom

FOR THE CAKE

1 stick (8 tablespoons) unsalted butter, melted, plus more for the pan

⅓ cup buttermilk

Marinate the prunes: Place the prunes in a large airtight container. In a medium saucepan, combine 4 cups water with the bay leaves, lemon peel, orange peel, cardamom pods, and cinnamon stick. Bring to a boil over high heat. Pour the liquid through a fine-mesh strainer into the container with the prunes. Discard the peels and spices. Pour the brandy into the prune mixture, then cover the container tightly. Let the prunes sit in the refrigerator for at least 24 hours or ideally up to 48 hours. Drain the prunes just before using.

Make the streusel: In the bowl of a stand mixer fitted with the paddle attachment, combine the rye flour, both sugars, the butter, salt, ground cinnamon, and ground cardamom. Mix on medium speed until it resembles bumpy sand, about 3 minutes. Set aside.

Make the cake: Preheat the oven to 350°F. Grease an 8-inch round cake pan with a little butter. Line it with parchment paper and grease again.

Whisk together the 8 tablespoons melted butter with the buttermilk, sour cream, eggs, and vanilla in a large bowl. Sift in the flour, granulated sugar, baking powder, salt, and baking soda. Stir until just combined, but don't overmix.

Pour half the batter into the cake pan. Scatter about three-quarters of the prunes over the batter. Add the remaining batter, scatter the rest of the prunes on top, then sprinkle on the streusel. Gently press down the streusel into the prunes and batter. Bake for about 1 hour,

RECIPE CONTINUES

Prune Coffee Cake (page 146)
and Cheesecake (page 148)

1 tablespoon sour cream

2 large eggs

1 tablespoon pure vanilla extract

1¾ cups all-purpose flour

1 cup granulated sugar

1½ teaspoons baking powder

1 teaspoon kosher salt

⅛ teaspoon baking soda

rotating halfway through, until a toothpick inserted in the center comes out clean. Let cool completely before cutting. Cover and store any leftovers at room temperature for up to 2 days.

This recipe was developed by Renee Hudson, the original pastry chef at Agi's Counter, and it's by far the most popular dessert we serve. It is a perfect cheesecake, so the cult following makes sense. Instead of reinventing the wheel, it felt important to me that we just nail a good old-fashioned slice that is ready for a Golden Girls–style gossip session. Any type of fruit compote (see pages 204–205) is perfect, but my favorite way to serve this cake is with a drizzle of great olive oil, a squeeze of lemon, and a pinch of flaky sea salt. It's life changing.

Serves 8

Cheesecake

FOR THE CRUST

1 stick (8 tablespoons) unsalted butter, plus more for the pan

¼ cup packed dark brown sugar

¾ teaspoon kosher salt

2½ tablespoons cornstarch

½ cup all-purpose flour

1 cup graham cracker crumbs

Preheat the oven to 325°F. Grease an 8-inch springform pan with a little butter. Line the bottom with a round of parchment paper and grease again.

Make the crust: In the bowl of a stand mixer fitted with the paddle attachment, beat the butter and brown sugar on medium speed until combined, about 2 minutes. Add the salt, cornstarch, flour, and graham cracker crumbs. Beat on low speed until just combined. Pack the crust into the bottom of the pan in an even layer. Bake for 10 to 15 minutes, until the crust is set and lightly golden brown. Remove from the oven and let cool completely.

Meanwhile, make the filling: Clean and dry the bowl and paddle, then return them to the stand mixer. Beat the cream cheese, cornstarch, and granulated sugar on medium speed until light and fluffy, about 5 minutes. Add the vanilla and eggs and beat on low speed until just combined, about 1 minute. Be careful not to overmix. Add the heavy cream and beat on low speed until the mixture just comes together and is no longer runny. Cover the bowl and let the filling sit at room temperature for 30 minutes to let the air bubbles rise to the surface.

Pour half the batter over the crust and gently tap the pan to release any air pockets. Finish pouring in the remaining batter. Place the springform in a roasting pan or casserole dish. Transfer to the oven but keep the door open. Fill a pitcher with water and pour it into the baking dish so it comes three-quarters of the way up the sides of the springform. Close the oven and bake for about 1½ hours, rotating halfway through, until the cheesecake is light golden brown and just slightly jiggly in the very center. Pull the cheesecake from the oven, but let it sit in the water bath until completely cooled. Remove from the water bath and refrigerate, uncovered, for 24 hours to fully set before serving. Cover and store any leftovers in the refrigerator for up to 2 days. The cake can also be wrapped tightly and frozen for up to 2 weeks. Defrost in the refrigerator for a day.

FOR THE FILLING

32 ounces cream cheese, room temperature, or 4 cups Fresh Cheese (page 201) or store-bought ricotta, room temperature and drained

5 tablespoons cornstarch

½ cup granulated sugar

2 tablespoons pure vanilla extract

4 large eggs

2 cups heavy cream

Carrot & Coriander Cake (page 153),
Szilvás Pite (page 152), and
Caraway Apple Cake (page 154)

This is one of the most traditional, recognizable cakes in Hungary. It's a simple and very rustic cake, a true home baker's dessert. The batter is really just a vehicle, so any stone fruit like peaches, apricots, nectarines, or even cherries work perfectly here. Just make sure you're using fruit in the peak of its season and especially any fruit that's gotten a little overly ripe.

Serves 6 to 8

Szilvás Pite (Plum Cake)

Unsalted butter, for greasing

1 cup all-purpose flour

1 teaspoon baking powder

½ teaspoon kosher salt

2 large eggs

1 cup plus 2 tablespoons sugar

1 cup plain full-fat Greek yogurt

⅓ cup canola oil

8 ripe plums, halved and pitted

1 vanilla bean, halved lengthwise and seeds scraped

1 teaspoon fennel seeds, lightly ground

Preheat the oven to 375°F. Grease a 9 × 13-inch baking dish with a little butter.

Whisk together the flour, baking powder, and salt in a large bowl. In a separate large bowl, whisk together the eggs and 1 cup of the sugar to make a thick pale yellow mixture. Add the yogurt and canola oil and whisk to combine. Whisk in the dry ingredients until a smooth batter forms. Transfer to the prepared pan. Arrange the plums over the surface, skin side up.

Mix together the remaining 2 tablespoons sugar, the vanilla seeds, and the ground fennel in a small bowl. Rub together with your fingers until thoroughly combined. Sprinkle the sugar mixture over the top of the cake. Bake for about 50 minutes, rotating halfway through, until a toothpick inserted in the center comes out clean. Let cool completely in the baking dish before serving. Cover and store any leftovers at room temperature for up to 2 days or in the refrigerator for up to 1 week.

I love carrot cake. I would even probably say it's my favorite cake. But surprisingly, it wasn't something I grew up eating very often. The few times I got to have it was at a tiny French bistro in Florida. Nana Arlene, my mom, and I would go and be ladies who lunch, with tiny teacups, croque madame, and slices of carrot cake. This cake brings back those memories but is updated with coriander, which accents the carrot flavor, and spelt and almond flours, which add a great body. It's a perfectly moist cake to be served with tea or even enjoyed as breakfast.

Serves 10

Carrot & Coriander Cake

Preheat the oven to 325°F. Grease a 9-inch round cake pan with a little butter and coat the sides with a handful of turbinado sugar, shaking it around the pan.

In the bowl of a stand mixer fitted with the paddle attachment, beat the butter with the granulated sugar, honey, orange zest, and coriander on medium speed until light and fluffy, about 5 minutes. Add the eggs, one at a time, stopping to scrape down the sides of the bowl after each addition. In a medium bowl, whisk together the spelt flour, almond flour, and baking powder. Add the dry ingredients to the wet ingredients and beat on low speed until just combined. Use a rubber spatula to fold in the grated carrot.

Transfer the batter to the prepared pan. Bake for 50 to 60 minutes, until a toothpick inserted in the center comes out clean. Cool for 1 hour in the pan before inverting the cake onto a wire rack to cool completely. Cover and store any leftovers at room temperature for up to 2 days or in the refrigerator for up to 1 week.

2½ sticks unsalted butter, softened, plus more for the pan

Turbinado sugar

1¼ cups granulated sugar

¼ cup honey

Zest of 1 orange

2 teaspoons ground coriander

4 large eggs

1½ cups spelt flour

1½ cups almond flour

2 teaspoons baking powder

2 large carrots, peeled and grated

This cake is great without frosting, but for an extra sweet touch whip a softened 8-ounce block of cream cheese with 3 tablespoons of confectioners' sugar until smooth and spread over the top. Garnish the frosting with unsweetened coconut flakes.

When I was growing up, the highlight of Rosh Hoshana, the Jewish New Year, was a fat slice of apple cake. It was a sweet and reliable part of the holiday. But as I got older and my palate developed, I started to feel like the cake fell a little flat. There was nothing playing with the apples to bring out some dimensionality. This version injects plenty of life with nutty rye flour, bittersweet caraway, and floral thyme. But the real force comes from root beer, which adds a strong and mysterious herbal note to the cake.

Serves 8

Caraway Apple Cake

10 tablespoons unsalted butter, softened, plus more for the pan

14 ounces Granny Smith apples, peeled, cored, and sliced (5 cups)

Zest and juice of 1 lemon

1 cup packed light brown sugar

3 large eggs

1½ cups root beer

1 cup plus 2 tablespoons all-purpose flour

1 cup rye flour

2 teaspoons baking powder

Kosher salt

Leaves from 5 fresh thyme sprigs

2 tablespoons caraway seeds, ground (see page 209)

2 tablespoons turbinado sugar

FOR THE THYME SYRUP

½ cup granulated sugar

8 fresh thyme sprigs

Preheat the oven to 325°F. Grease a 9-inch round cake pan.

Toss the apples with the lemon zest and juice in a large bowl. In the bowl of a stand mixer fitted with the paddle attachment, beat the butter and brown sugar on medium speed until light and fluffy, about 5 minutes. Add the eggs, one at a time, stopping to scrape down the sides of the bowl after each addition. With the mixer running on low speed, trickle in the root beer. Stop again to scrape down the sides of the bowl. In a large bowl, mix together the all-purpose flour, rye flour, baking powder, and large pinch of salt. Add to the wet ingredients and use a rubber spatula to stir until combined. Fold in the thyme leaves and caraway.

Pour the batter into the prepared cake pan. Fan the apples across the top of the cake and sprinkle the top with turbinado sugar. Bake for about 1 hour, until a toothpick inserted in the center comes out clean. Let the cake cool for 5 minutes before flipping onto a large plate. Set a cooling rack over the cake and use the plate to flip the cake again so the apples are facing up.

Make the thyme syrup: Combine the sugar, thyme sprigs, and ½ cup water in a small saucepan. Bring to a boil over high heat. Remove from the heat and brush the syrup generously over the top of the cake. Let cool completely before serving. Cover and store any leftovers at room temperature for up to 2 days or in the refrigerator for up to 1 week.

Carrot & Coriander Cake (page 153),
Caraway Apple Cake (page 154),
and Szilvás Pite (page 152)

Time for a second helping! Hungarian desserts are so colorful, creative, and inventive with unexpected surprises.

Desserts

Fennel, Orange & Chocolate Mandel
Bread (page 159), Vollmond (page 160),
and Kifli (page 161)

Mandel bread is the Jewish answer to biscotti, a twice-baked cookie meant to be enjoyed with coffee, tea, or alcohol. Nana Arlene was the pastry maker in the family and she worshipped at the altar of cookbook author Maida Heatter. Her favorite dessert was Maida's mandel bread with anise and apricot jam. My version uses fennel, orange, currants, and chocolate for a decadent-sounding cookie that's actually lighter than you would think. I'm also breaking with tradition in a big way. Instead of the double bake for a crunchy cookie, I like to stop after the first bake for one that's soft and more cake-like.

Makes about 30

Fennel, Orange & Chocolate Mandel Bread

Preheat the oven to 350°F. Line a rimmed baking sheet with parchment paper.

In the bowl of a stand mixer fitted with the paddle attachment, beat the butter and brown sugar on medium speed until light and fluffy, about 5 minutes. Add the eggs, one at a time, stopping to scrape down the sides of the bowl after each addition. Add the orange zest and vanilla and mix until just combined. In a medium bowl, whisk together the flour, baking powder, salt, and cinnamon. With the mixer on low speed, add the dry ingredients in two parts, waiting until the first part is fully incorporated before adding the next. Mix in the currants, chocolate, and fennel seeds. Use a rubber spatula to scrape down the sides and along the bottom of the bowl to make sure everything is incorporated.

Split the dough into 3 equal portions and shape each one into a log about 8½ × 4½ inches. Arrange all 3 logs on the prepared baking sheet, running perpendicular to the long edge, leaving about 1 inch between each one. Bake for 40 to 45 minutes, until the dough is puffed and set. Let cool completely on the baking sheet.

Transfer the logs to a cutting board and cut into 1-inch-thick slices, yielding about 30 pieces. Serve immediately or store in an airtight container at room temperature for up to 1 week. Alternatively, the cooled logs can be wrapped in plastic wrap and aluminum foil, then frozen for up to 3 months. Thaw overnight in the refrigerator, then bring to room temperature before slicing.

1½ sticks unsalted butter, softened

2¾ cups packed dark brown sugar

6 large eggs

2 tablespoons grated orange zest

2 tablespoons pure vanilla extract

5½ cups all-purpose flour

1 tablespoon baking powder

½ tablespoon kosher salt

¾ teaspoon ground cinnamon

1½ cups dried currants

3 ounces bittersweet chocolate (64%), chopped

2 tablespoons fennel seeds

This is a completely made-up cookie. Do not go to Hungary and ask for a vollmond—they'll think you're crazy. We make these at Agi's Counter, a sort of riff on the Austrian crescent cookies. While those are shaped like crescent moons, these little balls look like a full moon, or Vollmond in German. And instead of straight almond, these have plenty of lemon zest and anise seed to accent the flavor. The unfortunate part is they're so tiny and delicious, it's almost impossible to stop eating them.

Makes 30 cookies

Vollmond

2 sticks (½ pound) unsalted butter, room temperature

¼ cup granulated sugar

1 tablespoon anise seeds

Zest of 1 lemon

Kosher salt

1⅔ cups all-purpose flour

1 cup almond flour

TO GARNISH

Confectioners' sugar

In the bowl of a stand mixer fitted with the paddle attachment, beat the butter, granulated sugar, anise, lemon zest, and a big pinch of salt on medium speed until light and fluffy, about 5 minutes. Scrape down the sides of the bowl. In a medium bowl, whisk together the all-purpose flour and almond flour. With the mixer on low speed, add the dry ingredients in two parts, waiting until the first part is fully incorporated before adding the next. Wrap the dough tightly in plastic wrap and refrigerate for 1 hour to allow the dough to rest.

Preheat the oven to 325°F. Line two large rimmed baking sheets with parchment paper.

Unwrap the dough. Pinch off about a heaping tablespoon of dough, roll it into a ball between the palms of your hands, and set it on one of the prepared baking sheets. Continue pinching and rolling, spacing the balls about ½ inch apart. Once the first baking sheet is full, transfer to the oven while preparing the rest of the dough.

Bake for about 20 minutes, until lightly golden. Let cool for 5 minutes. (Meanwhile, start baking the second set of cookies.) Scoop some confectioners' sugar into a small bowl. Drop each warm cookie into the sugar and rotate it to coat, then transfer to a wire rack to cool completely. Store any leftovers in an airtight container at room temperature for up to 3 days.

These rolled crescent cookies, filled with some combination of jam, nuts, and chocolate, are a sweet holiday tradition in Hungary (but they can also be made savory with ingredients like poppy seeds and cheese). The dough is yeasted for a light and airy texture but loaded with butter for a soft flakiness, kind of like a combo of Pillsbury crescents and rugelach. They're perfect companions for coffee or tea, adding just the right amount of elegance.

Makes 16 cookies

Kifli

Make the dough: In the bowl of a stand mixer fitted with the paddle attachment, beat the butter on medium speed until light and fluffy, about 5 minutes. Add the flour. Use your fingers to pinch and rub the butter into the flour until a fine meal is formed. In a small bowl, combine the sour cream, egg yolks, sugar, yeast, and vanilla. Stir until the yeast has dissolved. Add the sour cream mixture to the flour mixture and mix on low speed until a shaggy dough forms, about 3 minutes, being careful not to overmix. Turn out the dough onto a work surface and use your hands to gather the dough until it comes together as a shaggy mass. Flatten into a rough disk, wrap tightly in plastic wrap, and refrigerate for 2 hours, until the dough is very firm.

Make the filling: After the dough has been chilling for 1 hour, vigorously whisk the egg whites in a large bowl until foamy, about 2 minutes. Fold in the walnuts, poppy seeds, sugar, and lemon juice. Cover with plastic wrap and let rest at room temperature for 1 hour while the dough finishes chilling.

Preheat the oven to 350°F. Line two large rimmed baking sheets with parchment paper.

Unwrap the dough and cut it in half. Rewrap and refrigerate the half you're not working with. Dust a work surface with a little flour and sprinkle some sugar on top. Use a rolling pin to roll out the dough into a 12-inch circle. Try to get the dough as thin as you can without breaking it. Use a pizza cutter or sharp knife to cut the circle into 8 even triangles. Scoop 1 tablespoon of filling onto the widest end of each triangle, about 1 inch from the edge. Gently pull the wide end

FOR THE DOUGH

2 sticks (½ pound) unsalted butter, room temperature

2½ cups all-purpose flour, plus more for the work surface

½ cup sour cream

2 large egg yolks

½ tablespoon sugar, plus more for the work surface and dusting

1 tablespoon active dry yeast

½ teaspoon pure vanilla extract

FOR THE FILLING

2 large egg whites

¾ cup finely chopped walnuts

1 tablespoon poppy seeds

3 tablespoons sugar

¼ teaspoon lemon juice

RECIPE CONTINUES

up and over the filling and then continue rolling tightly all the way to the tip. Transfer to the prepared baking sheet and repeat, arranging 8 cookies, evenly spaced.

Dust the top of the cookies with some more granulated sugar. Bake for 20 to 25 minutes, until lightly golden brown. Transfer to a wire rack. While the first batch bakes, roll and fill the remaining half of the dough and arrange on the second baking sheet before baking. Cool the cookies completely before serving. Store any leftovers in an airtight container at room temperature for up to 2 days.

Képviselőfánk, a simple choux dough baked until puffy, then filled with pastry cream and finished with confectioners' sugar, are a little bit of a mystery: not only are they not doughnuts, despite their name (they're more like profiteroles), there's no real traceable origin. The oral history is that they were served as snack cakes to members of parliament in the 1800s. But in contemporary times, they've become a popular treat for everyone to enjoy. The pastry cream here is heavy on lemon, but you can infuse it with whatever you like. Cardamom, chocolate, and rose water are all great.

Makes 18 "doughnuts"

Parliament Doughnut

Preheat the oven to 400°F and set two racks roughly in the center. Line two large rimmed baking sheets with parchment paper.

Make the choux: Bring the butter, salt, and 1 cup water to a boil in a small saucepan over medium heat. Remove from the heat and add all the flour. Mix with a wooden spoon until the flour is fully hydrated. Return to medium heat and continue to stir until the dough pulls away from the sides of the pan and forms a ball of dough (or it registers 175°F on an instant-read thermometer). There should also be a light film of dough that barely covers the pot.

Transfer the dough to the bowl of a stand mixer fitted with a paddle attachment. Mix on medium speed until the dough has cooled down slightly, about 5 minutes. Maintaining medium speed, add the eggs, one at a time, waiting until each is fully incorporated before adding the next. The dough might look like it's coming apart, but it'll pull together again. Once all the eggs are in, scrape down the sides of the bowl and mix again on high speed for 10 seconds to ensure the dough is fully combined. Transfer the choux to a piping bag or plastic zip-top bag.

To pipe the choux, cut a small opening in the piping or zip-top bag. Holding the bag at a slight angle, pipe a 2-inch-wide mound onto one of the prepared baking sheets. Lightly push down with the bag and pull away for a clean finish. Repeat with the remaining batter for a total of 9 mounds per sheet, evenly spaced with at least 3 inches between each mound. Use a wet finger to press down on each mound to smooth the top and eliminate bumps. Bake for about 25 minutes, until golden

FOR THE CHOUX

6 tablespoons unsalted butter

½ teaspoon kosher salt

1 cup all-purpose flour

4 large eggs

FOR THE PASTRY CREAM

5 large egg yolks

½ cup granulated sugar

3 tablespoons plus 2 teaspoons cornstarch

Kosher salt

2 cups whole milk

Zest of 2 lemons

2 tablespoons unsalted butter, cut into cubes

Juice of 1 lemon

TO GARNISH

Confectioners' sugar

RECIPE CONTINUES

brown and puffed. Turn off the oven and crack the door open. Let the pastry sit in the hot, dry air for 30 minutes. Remove from the oven and let cool completely before filling.

Make the pastry cream: Prepare an ice-water bath in a large bowl. Set aside.

Whisk together the egg yolks, granulated sugar, cornstarch, and a pinch of salt in a large bowl to make a thick, pale yellow mixture. In a medium saucepan, combine the milk and lemon zest. Set over medium heat until the milk just begins to steam, about 5 minutes. While whisking constantly, stream the warm milk into the egg mixture. Pour the mixture back into the saucepan and set back over medium heat. Cook, whisking occasionally, until the mixture has thickened significantly and begins to bubble, about 5 minutes. Once at a bubble, whisk vigorously for 1 minute. Remove from the heat and whisk in the butter. Immediately transfer the pastry cream to a medium bowl and set in the ice-water bath. Press plastic wrap directly on the surface of the custard to stop a skin from forming. Chill the custard for 30 minutes in the ice-water bath, then remove the bowl and continue to chill for 2 hours in the refrigerator. Right before using, whisk in the lemon juice. Transfer the cream to a piping bag or plastic zip-top bag.

To assemble, cut the doughnuts in half horizontally and separate the halves. Pipe about ¼ cup of pastry cream onto each bottom half, then gently press the top half on. Dust with confectioners' sugar right before serving. The doughnuts are best enjoyed right away.

If Hungary had American-style county fairs, these little fritters would be a staple. The name *thimbles* comes from Hungarian food writer George Lang, and I kept it because *thimbles* is more cute, whimsical, and fairy tale–like than what most Hungarians would call them: *fritters*. They're best rolled in sugar while still hot (the heat activates the fragrant caraway) and eaten fresh. The cheese makes them meltingly soft and tender, which means that if you eat one, you're probably going to eat a half dozen.

Makes 12 thimbles

Caraway-Sugared Thimbles

3 large eggs

1½ cups Fresh Cheese (page 201) or store-bought ricotta

1 vanilla bean, halved lengthwise and seeds scraped

¾ cup all-purpose flour

⅓ cup sugar

4 teaspoons baking powder

Kosher salt

Canola oil, for frying

FOR CARAWAY SUGAR

½ cup sugar

2 tablespoons caraway seeds, toasted and ground (see page 209)

Whisk together the eggs, cheese, and vanilla seeds in a large bowl. Sift in the flour, sugar, baking powder, and a big pinch of salt. Use a rubber spatula to fold everything together, being careful not to overmix. Cover loosely with plastic wrap and keep in a warm area for 2 hours until the dough becomes spongy.

Pour enough oil (likely about 2 quarts) into a large Dutch oven to reach a depth of 2 inches. Set over medium-high heat and bring to a temperature of 350°F on a deep-fry thermometer. Set yourself up with a rimmed baking sheet lined with paper towels. You'll also need a wide slotted spoon or spider strainer.

While the oil heats, make the caraway sugar: Combine the sugar and caraway seeds in a large bowl. Rub together with your fingers until thoroughly combined.

Working in batches, carefully lower 1-tablespoon scoops of batter into the hot oil, frying 3 or 4 scoops at a time; do not crowd the pan. Fry for about 3 minutes, until golden brown all over. They should flip over as they cook, but you might need to use the spoon to give them a nudge occasionally.

Once puffed and golden brown, use the spoon to transfer to the paper towels to drain. Repeat with the remaining batter, making sure the oil returns to 350°F. While the thimbles are still warm, toss in the bowl of caraway sugar until they're fully coated. Transfer the thimbles to a large plate and serve warm. The thimbles are best enjoyed right away.

My family back in Hungary—Agi's nephew and his partner—introduced me to this recipe. They make this when plums are at their peak, bursting with juices. Many central and eastern European countries have some version of this dumpling, and the fruit is interchangeable with apricots, peaches, or nectarines. It's a simple recipe of halved fruit that gets wrapped in potato dough, boiled, and rolled in sugared bread crumbs. The simplicity makes this beautiful, especially when you slice into the dumpling to find a purple arc.

Makes 8 dumplings

Szilvás Gombóc (Plum Dumpling)

FOR THE DUMPLINGS

2 large russet potatoes, peeled and cut into 1-inch pieces

½ cup cornstarch

½ cup all-purpose flour, plus more for the work surface

2 large egg yolks

4 ripe plums, halved and pitted

FOR THE BREAD CRUMBS

1 stick (8 tablespoons) unsalted butter

2 cups panko

½ cup granulated sugar

TO GARNISH

Whipped cream

Confectioners' sugar

Make the dumplings: Place the potatoes in a medium saucepan and cover with cold water. Bring to a boil over high heat and cook the potatoes for 10 to 15 minutes, until fork-tender. Drain thoroughly and let cool until safe to handle. Use a ricer or food mill to process the potatoes into a large bowl, or use a potato masher. Add the cornstarch, flour, and egg yolks. Using your hands, pinch and knead the dough into a smooth ball. Cover the bowl with a kitchen towel and set aside to rest for 10 minutes.

Make the bread crumbs: Melt the butter in a large saucepan over medium heat. Add the panko and cook, stirring frequently, until the bread crumbs are golden brown and toasted, about 4 minutes. Remove from the heat and transfer to a medium bowl to cool for 5 minutes. Add the sugar and toss to combine. Set aside.

Bring a large pot of water to a gentle boil over medium heat. Line a baking sheet or large plate with paper towels. While the water is heating up, dust a work surface with a little flour. Uncover the dough. Pinch off about a heaping tablespoon of dough and roll into a ball between the palms of your hands. Repeat with the remaining dough to make 8 balls. Use a rolling pin to roll each ball into a flat round, about 3½ inches. Dust with more flour as needed. Place 1 plum half in the center of a dough round. Bring the edges of the dough up and over the plum, pinching the seams tightly. Repeat with the remaining dough and plums.

Lower half the dumplings into the boiling water. Cook for 3 to 4 minutes, until they float to the surface. Remove with a slotted spoon and drain on the paper towels. Boil the second batch of dumplings. While they're still warm, roll the dumplings in the bread crumbs. Serve the warm dumplings with a dollop of whipped cream and a dusting of confectioners' sugar. The dumplings are best enjoyed right away.

This quick and easy dessert reminds me of the fruit cups my mom would make for my brother and me as kids. She would lightly mash fresh berries and leave them to macerate in sugar until they were rich and syrupy. Here, the addition of Tokaji elevates this idea into adulthood. The floral and honey notes of Tokaji accent the fresh strawberries and bring out their natural sweetness. Piled high in a bowl with a large swirl of whipped cream, this simple dessert feels surprisingly elegant.

Serves 4

Tokaji-Drenched Strawberries & Cream

Toss together the strawberries, Tokaji, vinegar, sugar, and vanilla bean (seeds and pod) in a large bowl. Cover with plastic wrap and refrigerate for at least 4 hours, until the strawberries are soft and macerated, or up to 24 hours.

When ready to serve, set a fine-mesh strainer over a medium bowl. Strain the strawberries, reserving the liquid in the bowl. Remove the vanilla pod and discard. (The vanilla pod can also be dried out and stored in a jar of sugar to create vanilla sugar for future uses.)

Whisk the heavy cream to soft peaks in a small bowl. Arrange the berries in a pretty serving bowl and dollop the cream on top. Pour the strained liquid into a gravy boat or small pitcher and serve on the side for drizzling. These are best enjoyed right away.

1½ pounds ripe strawberries, trimmed and cut in halves or quarters

3 tablespoons Tokaji*

1 teaspoon red wine vinegar or Chamomile Vinegar (page 194)

1 tablespoon sugar

1 vanilla bean, halved lengthwise and seeds scraped

½ cup heavy cream

*Serve with shots of Tokaji to sip too. See page 8 for more about Hungary's traditional dessert wine.

This traditional Hungarian dessert was Grandma Agi's secret weapon when she wanted to make my brother and me feel extra special. Madártej, which translates to "bird's milk," refers to the custard. In the classic preparation (and the way Agi made it), little floating islands of meringue are served in a pool of custard, like the French île flottante. My version veers away from that. Instead, I build it like a trifle, with layers of jam, meringue, and custard mingling together. Make it as messy-beautiful as possible, eat it with a tall spoon, and be a kid about it.

Serves 6

Madártej (Bird's Milk)

FOR THE CUSTARD

1½ cups whole milk

½ vanilla bean, halved lengthwise and seeds scraped

3 strips of orange peel

5 large egg yolks (save 4 whites for the meringue)

¼ cup sugar

Kosher salt

FOR THE MERINGUE

1 cup sugar

4 large egg whites

½ teaspoon cream of tartar

TO PLATE

2 cups jam, any flavor, store-bought or homemade (page 208)

Make the custard: Heat the milk, vanilla bean seeds and pod, and orange peels in a small saucepan over low heat until it just begins to steam, about 5 minutes. Remove from the heat and cover with a lid. Let the mixture steep at room temperature for at least 1 hour or up to 2 hours. Fish out the orange peels and vanilla pod. The peels can be discarded, but the vanilla pod can be dried out and then stored in a jar of sugar to create vanilla sugar for future applications.

Whisk together the egg yolks, sugar, and a pinch of salt in a large bowl to make a thick pale yellow mixture. Set the milk back over medium heat briefly until the milk just begins to steam again. While whisking constantly, stream the warm milk into the egg mixture. Pour the mixture back into the saucepan and return to medium heat. Cook, stirring continuously with a wooden spoon, until the mixture thickens and coats the back of the spoon, about 5 minutes. Immediately transfer the custard to a medium bowl and cover with plastic wrap, pressing it onto the surface so the custard doesn't form a skin. Refrigerate for 2 hours, until completely cool.

Make the meringue: Without stirring, combine the sugar and ½ cup water in a small saucepan. Set over medium heat and let the sugar dissolve (still no stirring) and begin to simmer until it reaches a temperature of 240°F on a candy thermometer, about 5 minutes.

Meanwhile, in the bowl of a stand mixer fitted with a whisk attachment, combine the egg whites and cream of tartar. Beat on high speed until soft peaks form, about 2 minutes. When the sugar syrup is ready, set

RECIPE CONTINUES

the mixer on low speed and slowly stream the syrup along the side of the bowl into the meringue. Raise the speed to high and continue to whip until stiff peaks form, about 2 minutes.

To plate: Line up six 8-ounce glasses or mason jars. Spoon some of the meringue into the base of each glass. Add 2 generous tablespoons of jam on top, then a drizzle of some custard. Repeat one more time with each layer. Finish each glass with a dollop of meringue before serving. The madártej are best enjoyed right away.

Nana Arlene's secret ingredient was My T Fine pudding, the star player in her chocolate cream pie. This recipe gets as close to the box as possible, with some slightly elevated ingredients to reward your efforts. Scooping this out of a glass reminds me of the simple pleasures of pudding cups as a kid. The pudding is great on its own, but I especially like it with a sprinkle of sea salt and dollops of softly whipped cream. It's a nice, casual dessert that still feels presentational, impressive, and, most of all, nostalgic.

Serves 4

"Mighty Fine" Chocolate Pudding

Whisk together the eggs and sugar in a large bowl until the mixture is thick and pale yellow. Add the cornstarch, cocoa, and a big pinch of salt. Whisk until completely combined. Bring the milk to a gentle simmer in a small saucepan over medium heat, then remove from the heat. While whisking constantly, stream the hot milk into the egg mixture. Pour the mixture back into the saucepan and return to medium heat. Cook, stirring continuously with a wooden spoon, until the mixture thickens and coats the back of the spoon, about 5 minutes. Remove from the heat and whisk in the chopped chocolate, heavy cream, butter, and vanilla.

To plate: Portion the pudding into 4 individual cups. Cover each with plastic wrap, pressing it onto the surface so the pudding doesn't form a skin. Refrigerate for at least 2 hours or up to 24 hours before serving. To garnish, sprinkle each portion with a little flaky salt and a dollop of whipped cream. Grate the piece of chocolate over the top. Cover and store any leftovers in the refrigerator for up to 1 week.

6 large eggs

½ cup sugar

¼ cup cornstarch

3 tablespoons cocoa powder

Kosher salt

2 cups whole milk

1 ounce bittersweet chocolate (64%), chopped

2 tablespoons heavy cream

2 tablespoons unsalted butter

1½ teaspoons pure vanilla extract

TO PLATE

Flaky sea salt

Whipped cream

1 ounce bittersweet chocolate (64%)

There's an art to making palacsinta, Hungarian crepes, and I feel like I could write an entire book on them. There are so many subtleties to the batter, timing, technique, keeping them warm, and filling them. I have such fond memories of Agi making palacsinta and using her bare hands to flip them in the pan. (I do it that way now too, much to the shock of my kitchen staff.) Agi would arrange a smorgasbord of cheeses, nuts, jams, and sauces. My brother, Jordan, doused his in cinnamon sugar, chocolate syrup, and apricot jam, rolled it up tight, and walked around eating it. Mine was garnished with delicate dollops, folded neatly, and eaten on a plate. The way you "csinta" says a lot about you. At the restaurant, we use our imagination for a seasonal rotation of flavors, from sweet to savory. This batter leans a little eggier for sturdiness, with plenty of seltzer to make the crepes airy and spongy, so they're ready to be filled with anything.

Makes 16 crepes

Palacsinta Americana
(Sweet Pancakes)

Make the crepes: Whisk together the flour, milk, seltzer, eggs, vanilla, and a big pinch of salt in a large bowl. Let the batter rest in the refrigerator for 30 minutes to set.

Set an 8-inch crepe pan or nonstick skillet over medium-high heat. Add a small scoop of butter to the pan, tilting to cover the surface. Ladle the crepe batter onto the pan, tilting so the batter covers the entire surface. Don't be afraid to add a little more batter if it needs it. Let the first side of the crepe cook for about 2 minutes. You'll know to flip when the sides of the crepe begin to peel up off the pan. Using a spatula (I like to use my fingers like Grandma Agi), flip the crepe over and continue to cook on the other side for less than a minute. The result should be a golden-brown crepe that looks like it has craters spattered about it. Your first crepe will most likely be a throwaway and that's normal. Every batch should get a practice run. Continue with the rest of the batter to make 12 crepes, stacking each one on the plate as they're done. Serve with any or all of the suggested toppings. Palacsinta are best enjoyed the same day.

FOR THE CREPES

4 cups all-purpose flour

4 cups whole milk

1¾ cups cold seltzer

8 large eggs

1½ tablespoons pure vanilla extract

Kosher salt

Unsalted butter, for greasing

TOPPINGS

Fresh Cheese (page 201)

Syrupy Walnuts (page 202)

Chocolate Rum Sauce (page 203)

Cinnamon sugar

Fruit compotes or jams (pages 206–208)

Cherry Caramel (page 204)

Whipped cream

Drinking culture in Hungary mostly involves sipping palinka (Hungarian moonshine) or knocking back a few shots, so this chapter explores the possibilities of Hungarian alcohols meeting Western cocktail culture.

Drinks

Sour Shirley (page 183),
Czech Mate (page 182), and
The Nightcap (page 183)

This cocktail is an homage to Papa Steve, Agi's husband, who was born in the former Czechoslovakia. Agi loves her cognac, but Papa Steve always kept his bottle of plum slivovitz nearby. This cocktail highlights the natural sweetness of slivovitz with honey, plum compote, and a splash of orange blossom water. It's a simple drink that feels just fancy enough to be special.

Makes 1 drink

Czech Mate

4 fresh basil leaves

1½ ounces slivovitz

½ ounce fresh lime juice

½ ounce honey syrup (recipe follows)

1 teaspoon Plum Compote (page 207)

1 dash orange blossom water

Muddle 3 of the basil leaves in a cocktail shaker until fragrant. Add the slivovitz, lime juice, honey syrup, plum compote, and orange blossom water and fill the shaker with ice cubes. Close tightly and shake vigorously until the outside of the shaker is frosty and very cold.

Strain the drink into your glass* and garnish with the remaining basil leaf.

TO MAKE THE HONEY SYRUP

Heat ½ cup water and ½ cup wildflower honey in a small saucepan over medium heat until the honey is dissolved. Store the syrup in an airtight container in the refrigerator until ready to use, up to 1 month. Makes about 1 cup.

*Chill your glass 1 hour or more before serving.

Agi never ends a dinner without a little coffee and a little cognac. This drink hits both in one glass and adds the sweet and nutty notes of amaretto, in a nod to the classic French Connection cocktail, plus a lemon peel for a nice perfume and some acidity to cut through the booze. I would never interrupt Agi's nightly ritual, but for the rest of us, this is the perfect digestif.

Makes 1 drink

The Nightcap

Fill a rocks glass with a few cubes of ice or a large cocktail ice ball. Pour the cognac, amaretto, and coffee liqueur into the glass and give a few stirs. Garnish with the lemon peel. Sweet dreams.

1 ounce cognac

1 ounce amaretto (preferably Disaronno)

¼ ounce coffee liqueur

1 lemon peel, to garnish

The classic Shirley Temple, which was the gateway "cocktail" for many of us, will always remind me of going to a bar or bat mitzvah, securing my drink, and sitting in the VIP section (which meant hiding under the tablecloths) with my cousins, acting like we were in a nightclub. I would ask the bartender for as many cherries as possible, which is the attitude I think Shirley demands. Even though this cocktail is made with adult ingredients, this is not the time for Luxardo cherries. Only violently red syrupy-sweet maraschino cherries are worthy of this cocktail.

Makes 1 drink

Sour Shirley

Fill a tall glass with ice. Pour in the cherry cordial, vodka, and soda. Stir with a straw or long spoon. Garnish with as many cherries as your inner child wants.

2 ounces sour cherry cordial

1½ ounces vodka

6 ounces lemon-lime soda

Maraschino cherries, to garnish

I didn't start drinking mulled wine until I met my best friend, Daniel, who introduced me to the German tradition of Glühwein. It felt like a big spectacle, and it was the only thing I wanted to drink all winter. This version is comfort in a cup, the perfect drink for getting sloshed next to a roaring fire. Roasting oranges in the oven helps bring out a caramelized bitterness that complements all the warm spices. Port and brown sugar round out the drink with a nice sweetness. Because of all the intense flavors, go for a red wine that's full-bodied and dry, like a Malbec, Cabernet Sauvignon, or anything from Hungary's Villány region.

Makes about 10 drinks

Mulled Wine

Preheat the oven to 350°F. Line a rimmed baking sheet with parchment paper.

Stud each orange with 2 cloves and arrange on the prepared baking sheet. Roast the oranges for about 1 hour, until caramelized (they will look like they are burning; this is fine). Let cool slightly.

While the oranges roast, start mulling the wine. Stir together the remaining ingredients plus 1¼ cups water in a large saucepan. Set over medium heat and bring to a boil. Reduce the heat to low and gently simmer for 30 minutes.

When the oranges are just cool enough to handle, slice them in half and squeeze them into the wine mixture. Put the orange bodies into the wine as well as the juice. Continue simmering over low heat for another 30 minutes.

Set a fine-mesh strainer over a large bowl and pour the wine through. Discard the solids and pour the wine back into the same saucepan. Keep over low heat, about 150°F, while serving.

5 medium navel oranges

10 whole cloves

1 (750 mL) bottle ruby port

1 (750 mL) bottle dry red wine

5 ounces Armagnac

1 lemon, halved

1¼ cups packed brown sugar

1 tablespoon grated peeled fresh ginger

½ tablespoon ground allspice

½ tablespoon ground nutmeg

This cocktail is from the garden and meant for the garden. It's refreshing, colorful, and the perfect thing to sip outside on a hot day. Garnish it with any herbs, greenery, or edible blossoms you have. This is also a perfect recipe to multiply and batch, so you can keep the drinks coming until the romping starts.

Makes 1 drink

Romping in the Garden

¼ ounce lovage simple syrup (recipe follows)

½ ounce fresh lemon juice

1½ ounces gin

1½ ounces cucumber juice (recipe follows)

Flaky sea salt

Very cold club soda

Chill a glass or mason jar ahead of time. Fill the glass with ice. Add the simple syrup, lemon juice, gin, cucumber juice, and a pinch of flaky salt to the glass and stir vigorously. Top off with club soda and serve immediately.

You can chill a large batch of this in a pitcher and pour over ice with a club soda topper. But remember, the cucumber juice is good for only 2 days in the refrigerator.

TO MAKE THE LOVAGE SIMPLE SYRUP

Combine 1 cup sugar, 1 cup fresh lovage leaves (you could use mint leaves instead), and 1 cup water in a small saucepan over high heat and bring to a boil. Once the sugar is dissolved, remove from the heat and let cool. Store the syrup in an airtight container in the refrigerator for up to 1 month. Makes about 1½ cups.

TO MAKE THE CUCUMBER JUICE

Roughly chop 2 English cucumbers and place them in a blender. Puree on high speed until completely liquid, about 2 minutes. Set a fine-mesh strainer over a medium bowl and pour in the cucumber puree. Use a ladle to press on the solids before discarding. You should have about 2 cups of juice. Cover and refrigerate for up to 2 days. Shake well before using.

Thumper is my made-up name for this style of drink, essentially a shrub, developed with my friend (and favorite bartender) Robb Hinds when I was opening Agi's Counter. In Hungary, there's a famous soda named Bambi, which was very popular in the 1950s and '60s and recently relaunched. So Thumper is my companion to Bambi, a more natural and zippier refresher packed with caraway, anise, and vinegar. This Thumper can be made nonalcoholic with ginger beer, boozy with prosecco, or somewhere in the middle with a combo of both.

Makes 1 drink

Caraway Thumper

FOR THE SHRUB

1½ tablespoons caraway seeds, lightly toasted and ground (see page 209)

3 or 4 whole star anise

1 cup sugar

½ cup apple cider vinegar

¼ cup red wine vinegar

TO FINISH

Ginger beer

Champagne or prosecco (optional)

Make the shrub: Combine the caraway, star anise, sugar, both vinegars, and 1 cup water in a large saucepan and set over medium-high heat. Stir until the sugar has dissolved and the mixture is just starting to simmer. Strain through a fine-mesh sieve into an airtight container. Discard the solids. Store the shrub in the refrigerator until ready to use, up to 2 months. Makes about 2¼ cups.

To finish: Fill a tall glass with ice. Add 1½ ounces of the shrub and top off the glass with ginger beer. If using champagne, add only 1 ounce of ginger beer and fill the rest of the glass with champagne.

Caraway Thumper (page 188) and
Romping in the Garden (page 186)

These are all the staple flavors of Hungarian cooking, reinvented with an update on flavors and techniques.

The Pantry

This hot sauce is like a traditional Hungarian eros pista but with a Mexican accent. I like the buttery and round flavors of guajillo chiles here, but morita are also great, a little smokier and spicier. The vibrant red adds a perfect splash of color and gentle heat to anything.

Makes 4 cups

Eros Pista (Hot Sauce)

2½ ounces dried guajillo or morita chiles

2 medium shallots, thinly sliced

2 garlic cloves, minced

2 cups canola oil

2 cups extra-virgin olive oil

Kosher salt

Put the chiles in a medium bowl and pour in enough boiling water to cover the chiles. Cover tightly with plastic wrap and let sit for 1 hour to rehydrate the chiles. Strain the chiles and remove and discard the stems and seeds. Combine the chiles, shallots, garlic, and canola oil in a large saucepan and set over low heat. Gradually heat the mixture, stirring occasionally, until fragrant and the shallots are translucent. Remove from the heat and let cool for 30 minutes, then stir in the olive oil. Ladle the mixture into a blender and blend on high speed until smooth. Season with plenty of salt. Store the sauce in an airtight container in the refrigerator for up to 1 month.

USE IT ON:
Dressed Deviled Eggs (page 14)
Pogácsa Morning Fried Egg Biscuit (page 42)
Bableves (page 62)
Unfaithful Roast Chicken (page 84)
Cucumber & Buttermilk Ranch (page 113)
Cauliflower Mush (page 129)

I was raised understanding that schmaltz was liquid gold, used only for special occasions like frying latkes or making chicken liver for holidays. But turning it into a mayo is a really fun way to use it and spread it around, literally. Schmaltz will be available at your butcher or most fine grocery stores, but you can also make your own by rendering chicken skin or saving the fat after searing thighs.

Makes 3 cups

Schmaltz Mayo

Combine the egg yolks, vinegar, mustard, lemon juice, and ice cubes in a blender. Blend on low speed until the ingredients are combined. Mix together the canola oil and schmaltz in a measuring cup with a pour spout. With the blender running on high speed, slowly pour in the fat combo until the mayo has emulsified and thickened. Store the mayo in an airtight container in the refrigerator for up to 1 week.

USE IT IN:
Dressed Deviled Eggs (page 14)
Turkey Club (page 51)
Confit Tuna Melt (page 50)
Agi's Counter Cabbage Slaw (page 108)

3 large egg yolks

¼ cup champagne vinegar or rice wine vinegar

3 tablespoons Dijon mustard

2 tablespoons fresh lemon juice

3 ice cubes

½ cup canola oil

¼ cup schmaltz (chicken fat), room temperature

This vinegar is a really cool staple to have in your pantry. It's a unique flavor profile to add to salad dressings, splash in a drink, spoon into borscht, or marinate fruit. Besides the lovely floral flavor, it also looks really pretty on the shelf.

Makes 2 quarts

Chamomile Vinegar

1 large bunch of fresh chamomile flowers

8 cups white balsamic vinegar

4 tablespoons raw wildflower honey

Stuff the chamomile in a 2-quart mason jar. In a large bowl, whisk together the vinegar and honey until the honey is completely dissolved. Pour the vinegar mixture over the chamomile and seal the jar tight. Let it sit in a cool, dry place at room temperature for 2 weeks before using. Refrigerate for up to 1 year. The longer it sits, the more flavor it will develop.

USE IT IN:
Pickled Beets (page 26)
Chilled Buttermilk Borscht (page 58)
Meggyleves (Sour Cherry Soup; page 61)
A Greek Salad (page 116)
Peaches & Cream (page 119)
Tokaji-Drenched Strawberries & Cream (page 171)

This is a science project and recipe rolled into one and it's super easy to make. As the mixture sits, the honey will turn runny and the garlic will mellow. It's incredibly versatile—I especially love it on chicken wings—with a sweet and savory flavor.

Makes 4 cups

Fermented Garlic Honey

Thoroughly clean and dry a 1-quart mason jar. Combine the honey and garlic in the jar and seal the jar tight. Let sit in a cool, dry place for 10 days, until the honey is very runny and bubbles are forming on the surface. Refrigerate for up to 3 months. The longer it sits, the more flavor it will develop.

4 cups very good raw honey

2 garlic cloves, smashed

USE IT ON:
Radish Kraut on Cornmeal Blini (page 22)
Lecsó (Marinated Blistered Peppers; page 33)
Pogácsa Morning Fried Egg Biscuit (page 42)
Savory Lángos (page 44)
Sweet Lángos (page 44)
Turkey Club (page 51)
Styrian Pumpkin Soup (page 63)
Turnip Schnitzel (page 79)
Unfaithful Roast Chicken (page 84)
Rántott Hús (Fried Pork Cutlet; page 89)
Carrots & Crispy Speck (page 126)

Every time you roast a chicken or eat wings or sear thighs, save the bones, clean them, and stockpile them in the freezer. All those bones will pay off with a great stock. The other secret to greatness starts with the vegetables. Take the time to cook them gently with enough salt to draw out the moisture—we're not going for color or caramelization. This will make a very delicate stock, slightly sweet from the veggies, thick and rich from the bones, and light in color.

Makes 5 quarts

Chicken Stock

5 pounds chicken bones, rinsed

1 stick (8 tablespoons) unsalted butter

2 medium yellow onions, roughly chopped

4 medium carrots, roughly chopped

4 celery stalks, roughly chopped

1 tablespoon kosher salt

1 tablespoon black peppercorns

1 bunch of fresh parsley

4 dried bay leaves

Place the rinsed chicken bones in a large stockpot and cover with cold water.

Heat the butter in a large skillet over low heat. Add the onions, carrots, celery, and salt. Gently cook the vegetables, stirring occasionally, for 10 to 15 minutes, until very soft but not taking on any color. Scrape the vegetables into the pot of chicken bones and add the peppercorns, parsley, and bay leaves. Bring to a boil over high heat. Use a spoon to remove any scum that develops on the surface, then reduce the heat to low and simmer for 6 hours. Continue topping off with water as needed to keep the bones submerged.

When the stock is rich and flavorful, pour through a fine-mesh strainer into several airtight containers. (I like to use quart containers labeled with the date.) Discard the solids. Cover and refrigerate the stock overnight to let the fat rise to the top. Peel the cold layer of fat off the top of the stock the next day. Refrigerate for up to 5 days or freeze for up to 6 months.

USE IT IN:
Bableves (page 62)
Styrian Pumpkin Soup (page 63)
Lorscht (Lamb Borscht; page 65)
Radish Soup & Semolina Dumplings (page 66)
Knot Soup (page 69)

Nokedli in Chicken Broth with So Much Dill (page 73)
Stuffed Cabbage (page 76)
Good Ol'-Fashioned Chicken Paprikash (page 82)
Rántott Hús (Fried Pork Cutlet; page 89)

Beans with Poppy Seeds, Pine Nuts & Fennel (page 109)
Poached Radishes (page 123)

Canned or boxed fish stock is great, but nothing beats the richness of a homemade stock. What's most surprising is it's quick and easy to make, usually under 30 minutes, unlike other types of stocks with long simmers. This one has a very delicate flavor profile and a light touch. Unless you're cooking whole fish frequently and saving the bones, go to the grocery and ask for bones at the fish counter.

Makes 2 quarts

Fish Stock

Combine the fish bones and salt in a large bowl. Cover completely with cold water and let sit for 1 hour to purge any blood or impurities. Drain and rinse the bones.

Heat the canola oil in a large Dutch oven over low heat. When the oil shimmers, add the onion, leek, fennel, celery, and garlic. Gently cook the vegetables, stirring occasionally, for 10 to 15 minutes, until very soft but not taking on any color. Add the fish bones and stir. Add the wine and reduce by half, about 6 minutes. Cover the ingredients with 8 cups cold water (or enough to submerge the bones). Add the parsley, bay leaves, and peppercorns. Bring to a gentle simmer and cook for 20 minutes. Skim off any scum that has gathered on the top using a large spoon or ladle. Pour the stock through a fine-mesh strainer into two airtight quart containers. (Don't forget to label with the date.) Cover and cool completely. Store the stock in the refrigerator for up to 1 week or in the freezer for up to 3 months.

USE IT IN:
Halászlé Túrós (Fisherman's Stew; page 100)

4 pounds fish bones (preferably from white-fleshed fish)

4 tablespoons kosher salt

4 tablespoons canola oil

1 large yellow onion, roughly chopped

1 large leek, rinsed well and roughly chopped

1 large fennel bulb, roughly chopped

4 celery stalks, roughly chopped

4 garlic cloves

2 cups dry white wine

1 bunch of fresh parsley

2 dried bay leaves

10 black peppercorns

A big slab of cured bacon is essential in any Hungarian household, a powerhouse flavor building block. It's a labor of love to cure your own bacon, but it's mostly inactive time. Just make room in the fridge and be patient while it sits. The payoff is having control over the quality, fat content, thickness of slices, and lack of preservatives.

Makes 5 pounds

Cured Bacon

5 pounds center-cut pork belly, skin on

¼ cup kosher salt

2 teaspoons pink curing salt

¼ cup packed dark brown sugar

Prepare the pork belly by rinsing it under cold running water and then patting it dry. Set the pork belly on a large rimmed baking sheet. Whisk together the remaining ingredients in a small bowl. Rub the belly with the salt mixture, then transfer the belly to a 2-gallon freezer bag and add any salt that has collected on the baking sheet. Refrigerate for 7 days, until the bacon is firm and dry. Set a wire rack in a large rimmed baking sheet. Remove the belly from the bag and place it on the rack skin side up. Air-dry uncovered in the refrigerator for 48 hours, until the exterior cures and darkens. Remove from the fridge 1 hour before cooking.

Preheat the oven to 200°F.

Transfer the entire baking sheet to the oven and cook the pork belly for about 2 hours, or until a digital thermometer inserted in the thickest part registers 150°F. Let cool completely before cutting. Wrap tightly with plastic wrap and store in the fridge for a week or freeze for up to 3 months.

USE IT IN:
Turkey Club (page 51)

I think it's really dreamy when fresh cheese, right out of the oven and still warm, is schmeared directly on bread. It's so transcendent. Having fresh farmer's cheese on hand immediately expands your pantry. Use it like you would ricotta, in both savory and sweet applications. Leaving milk and cream at room temp for a few days seems to go against all food safety logic, but the bacterial reaction creates lactic acid, curdles the milk, and starts the process. The cheese will be exposed to enough heat at the end of the process to kill off anything unwanted.

Makes 1½ pounds

Fresh Cheese

Combine the milk and heavy cream in a large Dutch oven. Cover and let sit at room temperature (around 70°F) for 60 to 72 hours. The curds should be visible. Try not to move the pot too much.

Preheat the oven to 300°F. Transfer the covered pot to the oven and bake for about 30 minutes, until the cheese has fully separated into curds. Remove the pot from the oven and let cool for 15 to 20 minutes. Line a mesh strainer with cheesecloth and pour the curds through. Let the cheese continue to strain for 30 minutes. Store the cheese in an airtight container in the refrigerator for up to 1 week.

9 cups whole milk

3 cups heavy cream

USE IT IN:
Cheesecake (page 148)
Caraway-Sugared Thimbles (page 166)
Palacsinta Americana (Sweet Pancakes; page 177)

Grandma Agi always had syrupy walnuts with palacsinta, but I find myself drizzling them on top of a lot of things. They're simple to make and great to have waiting in the fridge.

Makes 2 cups

Syrupy Walnuts

1 cup packed brown sugar

½ teaspoon kosher salt

4 tablespoons unsalted butter

⅔ cup heavy cream

1 cup chopped toasted walnuts (see page 209)

Flaky sea salt, crushed

Bring the brown sugar, salt, and ¼ cup water to a boil in a medium saucepan over medium heat. Boil for 3 to 4 minutes, until slightly thickened with thick bubbles. Add 2 tablespoons of the butter. Once the mixture starts to foam, quickly stir in the heavy cream and reduce to a low simmer. Cook for 3 more minutes, until the syrup is thick, like caramel. Remove from the heat. Stir in the remaining 2 tablespoons butter, the nuts, and some crushed flaky salt. Let cool completely in an airtight container before storing in the refrigerator for up to 1 month.

USE IT ON:
Lángos (Fried Bread; page 43)
Sesame Challah (page 52)
Pancake Torte (page 145)
Cheesecake (page 148)
Palacsinta Americana (Sweet Pancakes; page 177)

Hungarians love chocolate and they love liquor. Grandma Agi used to stir cognac into Hershey's syrup for a runny, boozy sauce. This is a slightly more proper way to pull it all together, but it has a similar spirit of fun. I like to keep a whole jar in the fridge for anything that needs something special, even if it's just a scoop of ice cream.

Makes 2 cups

Chocolate Rum Sauce

Put the chocolate in a medium bowl. In a small saucepan over medium heat, warm the heavy cream and brown sugar until the mixture just begins to steam. Pour over the chocolate. Let sit for 1 minute, then whisk until smooth. Add the rum and vanilla, whisking to combine. Cool to room temperature before serving. Store any leftover sauce in an airtight container in the refrigerator for up to 1 month.

12 ounces bittersweet chocolate (64%), chopped

1 cup heavy cream

4 tablespoons light brown sugar

½ cup dark rum

2 teaspoons pure vanilla extract

USE IT ON:
Lángos (Fried Bread; page 43)
Challah French Toast (page 54)
Golden Dumpling Cake (page 141)
Pancake Torte (page 145)
Cheesecake (page 148)
Fennel, Orange & Chocolate Mandel Bread (page 159)
Parliament Doughnut (page 163)
Caraway-Sugared Thimbles (page 166)
Tokaji-Drenched Strawberries & Cream (page 171)
Madártej (Bird's Milk; page 172)
Palacsinta Americana (Sweet Pancakes; page 177)

This is great to have on hand for a lot of uses, both sweet and savory. It's like an Italian agrodolce, a little tart and nicely sweet. Rehydrating the cherries in tea deepens the flavor of the caramel with a nice floral note.

Makes 1 quart

Cherry Caramel

4 cups dried cherries

1 sachet of tea (chamomile or green tea)

2 cups sugar

1 cup red wine vinegar

Place the cherries in a 1-quart container with the tea sachet. Cover with scalding hot water so the cherries are completely submerged. This can be done at least 2 hours or up to 1 day in advance. Drain the cherries, reserving ½ cup of the tea liquid.

Pour the sugar into a large heavy-bottomed saucepan. Shake the pan so the sugar spreads out evenly. Set over low heat and keep an eye on the sugar as it begins to caramelize and bubble around the edges. Once the sugar has completely caramelized, it will be a deep amber, 10 to 15 minutes in total. Remove from the heat momentarily and add the vinegar. The sugar will seize up, but don't be scared. Set over medium heat and bring the mixture to a simmer. Continue cooking until the sugar has dissolved into the vinegar. Add the cherries and the reserved tea liquid. Continue to cook for 8 to 10 minutes, until the caramel has thickened slightly. Remove from the heat and let cool completely. Store the caramel in a clean jar or other airtight container in the refrigerator for up to 3 months.

USE IT ON:

Chicken Liver Mousse (page 17)

Lángos (Fried Bread; page 43)

Turkey Club (page 51)

Challah French Toast (page 54)

Pork Chop with Lecsó & Onions (page 87)

Rántott Hús (Fried Pork Cutlet; page 89)

Peaches & Cream (page 119)

Golden Dumpling Cake (page 141)

Pancake Torte (page 145)

Cheesecake (page 148)

Parliament Doughnut (page 163)

Caraway-Sugared Thimbles (page 166)

Madártej (Bird's Milk; page 172)

Palacsinta Americana (Sweet Pancakes; page 177)

At Agi's Counter, we used to serve pickled grapes on the chicken liver mousse . . . until they migrated to the borscht instead, which shows how versatile they are. The vinegar highlights the natural acidity of green grapes and softens the snap into a soft, plump orb.

Makes 1 quart

Pickled Grapes

Pluck the grapes off the stems and wash thoroughly. Pat dry, then place them in a 1-quart mason jar.

Combine the vinegar, sugar, peppercorns, cinnamon stick, bay leaf, and ¼ cup water in a small saucepan over medium heat. Bring the ingredients to a simmer until the sugar has dissolved, then carefully pour over the grapes. Let the mixture cool, then tightly cover the jar and refrigerate for at least 24 hours before using, or up to 1 month.

1 pound seedless green or red grapes

1 cup white balsamic vinegar

1 cup sugar

¼ teaspoon black peppercorns

1 cinnamon stick

1 bay leaf

USE IT ON:
Chicken Liver Mousse (page 17)
Chilled Buttermilk Borscht (page 58)

This compote always reminds me of Violet Beauregarde in *Willy Wonka* because of the very plump blueberries, ready to burst, suspended in a shiny purple sauce. The coriander works in the background without being super present; it just brings forth a classic blueberry flavor.

Makes 4 cups

Blueberry Coriander Compote

4 pints fresh blueberries

⅔ cup sugar

1 tablespoon ground coriander

1 tablespoon fresh lemon juice

Combine 2 pints of the blueberries with the sugar, coriander, and lemon juice in a medium saucepan over medium heat and simmer, stirring occasionally, until the blueberries burst and the jam is starting to thicken, about 10 minutes. Transfer the mixture to a blender and blend on high speed until smooth. Set a fine-mesh strainer over a medium bowl. Pour the blueberry mixture through the strainer, pressing to release the liquid. Discard the solids. Let cool completely, then fold in the remaining 2 pints of blueberries. Store the compote in a clean jar or other airtight container in the refrigerator for up to 1 week.

USE IT ON:
Lángos (Fried Bread; page 43)
Country Club Crackers (page 46)
Challah French Toast (page 54)
Golden Dumpling Cake (page 141)
Pancake Torte (page 145)
Cheesecake (page 148)
Caraway-Sugared Thimbles (page 166)
Madártej (Bird's Milk; page 172)
Palacsinta Americana (Sweet Pancakes; page 177)

Stone fruit is a staple of Hungarian crops, so most Hungarians have plenty of compotes in their pantry. Plum has always been my favorite, sweet and just a little tart. This is a perfect time to use up any overly ripe, mushy fruit.

Makes 4 cups

Plum Compote

In a large saucepan, sprinkle the sugar in an even layer. Set over low heat and cook the sugar until a light amber caramel forms, about 6 minutes. Stir only occasionally. Deglaze the caramel with the port wine. Using a long-stemmed lighter, ignite the port and burn off the alcohol until the flames have subsided, about 1 minute. Carefully add in the plums, vanilla, and honey. Cook down until thick and sticky, 30 to 45 minutes. Remove from the heat and cool completely. Store the compote in a clean jar or other airtight container in the refrigerator for up to 1 week.

½ cup sugar

1 cup port wine

1 pound plums, halved and pitted

1 vanilla bean, split

2 tablespoons honey

USE IT ON:
Lángos (Fried Bread; page 43)
Country Club Crackers (page 46)
Challah French Toast (page 54)
Golden Dumpling Cake (page 141)
Pancake Torte (page 145)
Cheesecake (page 148)
Caraway-Sugared Thimbles (page 166)
Madártej (Bird's Milk; page 172)
Palacsinta Americana (Sweet Pancakes; page 177)

I developed this recipe with my friend and sous chef, Sara Pagan. The key to this jam is letting the rhubarb gently steam in a double boiler, which preserves the beautiful pink blush of the stalks. This delicate treatment will give you a vibrant and flavorful jam.

Makes 4 cups

Rhubarb Jam

5 pounds rhubarb, cleaned and cut into 1-inch pieces

2¼ cups sugar

½ cup fresh lemon juice (from 2 to 3 lemons)

Place the rhubarb in a medium metal bowl. Cover the top of the bowl tightly with plastic wrap and set over a large saucepan of water (the bowl shouldn't touch the water). Bring the water to a bare simmer over low heat. Let the rhubarb cook for 30 minutes, then transfer the rhubarb and its juices to a large saucepan. Add the sugar and lemon juice. Set over medium heat and continue to cook, stirring occasionally, for 25 to 30 minutes, until the rhubarb is broken down and the jam is starting to thicken. Remove from the heat and transfer to a clean jar or other airtight container. Let cool completely before storing in the refrigerator for up to 3 months.

USE IT ON:
Lángos (Fried Bread; page 43)
Country Club Crackers (page 46)
Challah French Toast (page 54)
Golden Dumpling Cake (page 141)
Pancake Torte (page 145)
Cheesecake (page 148)
Caraway-Sugared Thimbles (page 166)
Madártej (Bird's Milk; page 172)
Palacsinta Americana (Sweet Pancakes; page 177)

ON TOASTING NUTS & SEEDS

Recipes throughout this book rely on toasted nuts and seeds because toasting is by far the best way to use these ingredients. The slow and steady application of heat activates aromatic oils to concentrate all the natural flavor, making them more present in the final dish. Here's a rough guide on how I like to toast both.

Toasting Nuts

Preheat the oven to 350°F. Spread the nuts evenly on a rimmed baking sheet. Tender nuts, like pistachios and walnuts, will take 6 to 8 minutes. Dense nuts, like almonds, will take 8 to 10 minutes. In both cases, halfway through the baking time, pull the baking sheet out and give the nuts a good toss. Ultimately, you're looking for a rich and fragrant aroma with barely any color. Immediately transfer the nuts to a plate to cool completely, then use whole or chop as needed. Store any extra nuts in an airtight container at room temperature for up to 2 days.

Toasting Seeds

Set a small skillet over medium heat until warm. Add the seeds and shake into an even layer. Continue to shake occasionally as the seeds toast, 2 to 3 minutes. Just like the nuts, you're looking for a very fragrant aroma with barely any color. Transfer the seeds to a bowl to cool completely. To grind the seeds, I prefer using a mortar and pestle so I can control the texture. Pulsing in an electric spice grinder works too. And if you don't have either of those, do what my grandmothers have always done: pour the seeds into a plastic zip-top bag, seal it tightly, and beat it with a rolling pin.

These are some of the moments that I like to pause in my memory. They're the remedies, the recipes made by heart, that comforted me and brought me the most joy.

Remedies

As a child, I created a whimsical, fantastical world in my head, and Grandma Agi was at the center of my magical fantasy. She called me csillag, the Hungarian word for star, which made me sparkle inside. She would draw pictures of fairy-tale characters wearing elaborate costumes. She had a magic power in her that encouraged me to imagine and play.

Anytime my parents dropped me off at Agi's, I knew I'd be handed a cold chocolate fizz the second I passed the threshold. Agi would put on *Mary Poppins*, somehow the only VHS she seemed to own. I would lie on her huge black leather couch, my legs falling in every direction, and my magic fizzy potion made my cares drop away.

These are the secrets to a perfect chocolate fizz: use U-Bet syrup if you can find it, make sure the club soda and milk are both freezing cold, and have your favorite movie at the ready.

Serves 1

Chocolate Milk Fizz & *Mary Poppins*

Chocolate syrup (preferably U-Bet or, in a pinch, Hershey's)

½ cup very cold whole milk

¾ cup very cold club soda

Tilt a tall drinking glass on its side with one hand and pour in the chocolate syrup with the other. Twirl the glass as you pour so the chocolate coats all sides. Use as much chocolate as you desire, there's no correct measurement here. Place the glass on a saucer as it will overflow, which is part of the whimsy of this drink. Add the milk and top off with the club soda. Use a spoon to stir the drink aggressively so it begins to foam over the top of the glass. Serve with a straw and VHS copy of *Mary Poppins*.

MAGNAVOX

VHS HQ

POWER-ON

STANDBY-ON

HDMI

REW   F.FWD   STOP/EJECT   PLAY   RECORD   IR

4 HEAD HI-FI STEREO

HIGH GRADE

My mom has been making her banana bread ever since I can remember. Or, I should say, my mom has been perfecting her banana bread ever since I can remember. It's a lifelong project with no signs of stopping. Anytime someone mentions banana bread, her ears perk up and she's eager to compare notes. This recipe is her most up-to-date draft.

When I go visit, there's always banana bread at the ready. Nothing has sparked as many deep talks with Mom about life, my biggest worries, my joys and pains. Just like her love, it's always been there and there's a comfort in knowing it will always be there. Big things always happen over Mom's banana bread.

Makes one 13-inch loaf*

Mom's Banana Bread

4 sticks (1 pound) unsalted butter, room temperature, plus more for the pan

2 cups sugar

4 large eggs

1½ teaspoons pure vanilla extract

3 cups all-purpose flour

1 tablespoon baking soda

2 teaspoons ground cinnamon

2 cups very ripe bananas, mashed (about 4 bananas)

1 cup full-fat buttermilk

1 cup walnuts, crushed (optional)

6 ounces semisweet chocolate (64%), chopped (optional)

Preheat the oven to 350°F. Grease a 13-inch loaf pan with a little butter. Line with parchment paper, leaving some hanging over the sides, and grease the parchment.

In the bowl of a stand mixer fitted with the paddle attachment, cream the butter and sugar on medium speed until light and fluffy, stopping to scrape down the sides of the bowl, about 3 minutes. Add the eggs, one at a time, letting each one fully incorporate before adding the next. Beat in the vanilla.

Sift the flour, baking soda, and cinnamon onto a large piece of parchment paper. With the mixer running on low speed, add one-third of the dry ingredients, then roughly one-third of the banana and one-third of the buttermilk and mix until combined. Scrape down the sides of the bowl. Repeat the process two more times until everything is added and thoroughly combined. Mix in the walnuts and chocolate, if using.

Scrape the batter into the prepared pan and smooth the top. Bake for about 1½ hours, until a toothpick inserted in the center comes out clean. Let sit in the loaf pan for 1 hour at room temperature. Pull the overhanging parchment to move the loaf to a wire rack. Let cool completely before cutting.

*My mom makes a long loaf, but if you don't have a 13-inch pan, divide the batter between two 8 × 4-inch loaf pans instead.

Passover is to matzoh as Easter is to Cadbury. But my mom loves to buck the rules and snack on matzoh with schmears of butter and salt all year long. She sometimes made matzoh brie (scrambled eggs with crumbled matzoh) for Sunday breakfast and it always felt like a special occasion. It might sound odd to sprinkle cinnamon sugar on top of eggs, but it really does take it to an amazing place of deep comfort.

I especially remember one morning when she made it for my brother and me before school. It was a little disorienting, having such a rare delicacy on a random weekday. But the flood of sunny, lazy Sunday-morning joy filled me up and I couldn't shake the incredible feeling all day.

Serves 2

Matzoh Brie

Break up the matzoh into large shards. Place them in a medium bowl and submerge in cold water. Let the matzoh soak for about 1 minute, until soft. Drain the matzoh and gently squeeze out the water. In the same bowl, whisk the eggs, then add the matzoh and a pinch of salt to the eggs.

In a small bowl, stir the sugar and cinnamon together.

Melt a good knob of butter in a nonstick skillet over medium-high heat until it begins to bubble. Add the egg mixture. Use a rubber spatula to push the eggs around the pan until they begin to scramble but aren't too firm, 2 to 3 minutes. Divide between two plates and sprinkle with the cinnamon sugar.

2 sheets of matzoh

4 large eggs

Kosher salt

1 tablespoon sugar

½ teaspoon ground cinnamon

Unsalted butter

Agi used to make this old Ashkenazi remedy when my dad was little, whenever he was sick or just needed a pick-me-up. The mythos of kogel mogel is that the egg is for the body; the sugar is for the soul. To me it feels like the beginning of a custard or a cake when you whip the eggs and sugar together and want to lick the whisk.

Agi made it for me only a few times—soup was her go-to solution by then—but it felt so good to have this special gift passed through the generations of not just my family but my entire heritage too. I can confirm the healing properties are real.

Serves 1

Kogel Mogel

2 large egg yolks

1 teaspoon sugar

2 teaspoons cocoa powder (optional)

Soft whipped cream (optional)

Whisk together the egg yolks, sugar, and, if using, cocoa powder in a small bowl until light and airy, about 2 minutes. The sugar should completely dissolve. Serve with an optional dollop of whipped cream and a spoon.

This is Nana Arlene's signature comforting cake. It's not what most people think of as a traditional German chocolate cake, but it's the version I grew up with. No one (including Nana Arlene) knows where she got this recipe from; she's just been making it forever. She probably ripped it out of a magazine decades ago, but as far as I'm concerned, it belongs to her. When I asked her for the recipe, she wrote back and said, "I hope it comes out OK. I'm sure with you baking it, it will be great. Love you so so much."

When I think about this cake, what I remember is the distinctive aroma, which makes the entire house smell like the fluffiest, warmest chocolate cake you'll ever have. What I also remember are some pretty upsetting moments, like my parents' divorce or my brother going to rehab. But what I remember most of all is the way my nana reached out to care for me. She wrapped me in her love and set a slice of cake in front of me, her special way of placing a Band-Aid on the problem.

Serves 8 to 10

Nana's German Chocolate Cake

3 sticks (¾ pound) unsalted butter, plus more for the pan

8 ounces semisweet chocolate (64%), chopped

1 cup whole milk

2 tablespoons white distilled vinegar

2¼ cups sugar

3 large eggs

2 teaspoons pure vanilla extract

3 cups all-purpose flour

1½ teaspoons baking soda

½ teaspoon kosher salt

Preheat the oven to 350°F. Grease an 8-inch Bundt pan with a little butter.

Combine the 3 sticks butter and the chocolate in a large bowl. Fill a small saucepan just under halfway with water. Set it over medium heat until the water just begins to steam. Set the bowl of chocolate over the saucepan, making sure it doesn't touch the water. Stir frequently until the butter and chocolate are melted and smooth, about 4 minutes. Remove from the saucepan and set aside to cool slightly.

Meanwhile, stir together the milk and vinegar in a small bowl. Whisk the sugar, eggs, and vanilla into the chocolate mixture. Sift in the flour, baking soda, and salt, then pour in the soured milk. Stir together until just combined. Pour the batter into the prepared pan and tap a few times on your kitchen surface to even out the batter and release any air bubbles. Bake for 40 to 50 minutes, until a toothpick inserted comes out clean. Immediately invert onto a wire rack and let cool completely.

Cognac was a staple in the Salamon household. Agi kept the everyday bottle in the cupboard and the nice bottle in her china cabinet, tucked in the back corner behind her good plates.

On special occasions, the nice bottle would come out and my grandparents and dad would finish their meal with tiny crystal glasses of cognac alongside bowls of nuts, fruit, and chocolate. I felt special just being in the presence of such luxury, and time seemed to slow down.

On less special occasions, my grandparents would sit on their lawn chairs together and sip small glasses of the everyday stuff while my cousins and I played. I didn't appreciate it then, but now I understand the extraordinary lives my grandparents had, the war they both survived, the new life in a foreign country they built. It must have felt incredible to sit together and watch their family stretch on into the second generation.

Serves 1

A Swig of Cognac

Sit down. Pour yourself a glass. Enjoy.

1 bottle good cognac
(I prefer it a little chilled)

Your best and prettiest glass

Some chocolate, nuts, or fruit

Acknowledgments

This book is a home. A place where you want to nestle up in its corners and live in it for a while. Building that home took a village though. A village that has filled these pages with an abundance of love and care. I'd like to thank the following . . .

Casey Elsass, my overall loving cookbook doula fairy godfather. Thank you for helping me turn this dream into a reality.

Maeve Sheridan, mystical magical builder of worlds. I'm so lucky to have had your whimsy grace these pages.

Ed Anderson, my dream photographer. I still can't believe you said yes. It could not have been anyone else.

Spencer Richards, your whipped cream dollops are the stuff of legend, as is your skill to create architecture and story through food.

Jessica Quinn, my Jewish Latvian Ukrainian pastry sorceress. Thank you for being my loudest cheerleader. PS, I'm sorry about the carrot cake.

Athena Bochanis, I'm so glad we crossed paths on East Sixth Street all those years ago. Your expansive knowledge and understanding of Hungarian wines is truly a gift to both this book and myself.

Max Sinsheimer, thank you for seeing what I saw so early on: a purpose for this book.

Deb Brody, **Jacqueline Quirk**, **Stephanie Fletcher**, and **the HarperCollins/Harvest family**, thank you for taking a chance on the thirteen-year-old kid from South Florida who loved to collect cookbooks. He's waited the better part of thirty years for this moment.

Mom, **Dad**, and **Jordan**, thank you for dreaming with me. Every step of the way.

And most of all, Michael, my bee charmer. It is the greatest privilege of my life to love and to be loved by you.

A League of Extraordinary Women

Sara Pagan

Dorette Snover

Sharon DeFren-Moss

Julie Salamon

Lily Salcman

Lea Loustanau

Liz Salaway

Cookie

Emma Saias

Marilyn Saias

Agi Salaway

Frieda Ackerman

Lee Nissam

Suzanne Perrotto

Universal Conversion Chart

Oven temperature equivalents

250°F = 120°C	
275°F = 135°C	
300°F = 150°C	
325°F = 160°C	
350°F = 180°C	
375°F = 190°C	
400°F = 200°C	
425°F = 220°C	
450°F = 230°C	
475°F = 240°C	
500°F = 260°C	

Measurement equivalents

Measurements should always be level unless directed otherwise.

⅛ teaspoon = 0.5 mL

¼ teaspoon = 1 mL

½ teaspoon = 2 mL

1 teaspoon = 5 mL

1 tablespoon = 3 teaspoons = ½ fluid ounce = 15 mL

2 tablespoons = ⅛ cup = 1 fluid ounce = 30 mL

4 tablespoons = ¼ cup = 2 fluid ounces = 60 mL

5⅓ tablespoons = ⅓ cup = 3 fluid ounces = 80 mL

8 tablespoons = ½ cup = 4 fluid ounces = 120 mL

10⅔ tablespoons = ⅔ cup = 5 fluid ounces = 160 mL

12 tablespoons = ¾ cup = 6 fluid ounces = 180 mL

16 tablespoons = 1 cup = 8 fluid ounces = 240 mL

Index

About the Authors

Jeremy Salamon is the James Beard–nominated chef and owner of the beloved Agi's Counter in Brooklyn, a 2022 pick for *Bon Appétit*'s Best New Restaurants list and a 2023 Michelin Bib Gourmand award recipient. He began his career working under celebrated chefs in restaurants such as Locanda Verde, Prune, Buvette, and Via Carota, before becoming the executive chef of Manhattan restaurants the Eddy and Wallflower. He's been recognized by publications such as the *New York Times*, *Food & Wine*, *Forbes*, *The New Yorker*, Eater, *Travel + Leisure*, the Infatuation, and more. He lives in Brooklyn, New York, with his partner, Michael, and their cat, Sage. This is his first cookbook.

Casey Elsass is a food writer, recipe developer, and cookbook author living in Brooklyn, New York.